ECONOMIC DEVELOPMENT PROGRAMS FOR CITIES, COUNTIES, AND TOWNS

ECONOMIC DEVELOPMENT PROGRAMS FOR CITIES, COUNTIES, AND TOWNS

John M. Levy

PRAEGER

PRAEGER SPECIAL STUDIES • PRAEGER SCIENTIFIC

Library of Congress Cataloging in Publication Data

Levy, John M.
   Economic development programs for cities, counties,
and towns.

   Bibliography: p.
   Includes indexes.
   1. Urban policy--United States. 2. Community development, Urban--United States. 3. Federal aid to community
development--United States. I. Title.
HT123.L39   338.973   81-2716
ISBN 0-03-057891-4   AACR2

Published in 1981 by Praeger Publishers
CBS Educational and Professional Publishing
A Division of CBS, Inc.
521 Fifth Avenue, New York, New York 10175 U.S.A.

© 1981 by Praeger Publishers

123456789   145   987654321

Printed in the United States of America

To Lucie

PREFACE

This volume is intended as a practical guide for the student of economic development and for the beginning practitioner. It focuses on economic development programs for cities, counties, towns, and other small geographic entities. No attempt is made to discuss regional economic development. At the other end of the scale, no attempt is made to discuss economic development at the neighborhood level or the specialized area of downtown redevelopment. These exclusions reflect the author's preference for confining the work to that with which he has had direct experience. The particular emphases of the book stem largely from the writer's perceptions of what he would have found useful as a beginning practitioner.

The extensive discussions of the political side of economic development reflect the fact it is a highly political activity. It has a high degree of public visibility and a great sensitivity to the way the political winds blow. Public-relations and marketing aspects are discussed in detail because they are an integral part of the work of the economic developer. Indeed, the economic developer is likely to spend more of his time on these two items than on all other activities combined. Economic development in the United States is highly competitive, for there are far more communities seeking new industry than there are firms seeking new locations. This competitiveness, combined with the fact that business-location decisions are inevitably made under conditions of partial ignorance, makes skill in marketing, advertising, and public relations central elements for the successful development effort.

Development financing is discussed in some detail for rather obvious reasons. At some point in a serious conversation between firm and developer, the question "what can you do for us?" will often arise. And while it may be true that the pattern of economic development in the United States would not be greatly different if no jurisdiction or agency could offer financing incentives, the fact is that, given the competitiveness of economic development and the prevalence of financial tools available, no economic developer can afford to be ignorant of them.

Where technique and economic theory are discussed, the emphasis is placed upon methods which are not overly time consuming, and which can be used by the development practitioner or local official without a large staff or a large supply of funds for consultant services.

Thus the model of the local economy presented here is a simple export-base one—a model which can be easily comprehended and readily used in the design and subsequent explanation of the program. Some of the more elegant models to be found in texts on urban and regional economics are not mentioned. This is because the present author regards them not as less valid, but rather, as less practical. For this reason, there is, for example, no discussion of the input-output model. Its data needs and mathematical complexity place it beyond the practical reach of all but a few large and well-financed agencies.

In the discussions of marketing, the emphasis is placed upon judgments which can be made from readily available statistics, from measures which can be easily developed from such statistics, or from ordinary observations. More elegant techniques, such as mathematically complex accessibility models, are omitted, not because of questions of validity, but because of questions of practicality.

The final chapter of the book, on fiscal-impact analysis, presents a rather lengthy but, the writer hopes, readily comprehensible list of items for the economic developer to consider in gauging fiscal impact. This is followed by a simple model suggesting how the additional costs and revenues of new development can be evaluated. The model is such that a day or two of work with a hand calculator should be sufficient to generate rough but usable results.

Finally, a word about a thread that runs throughout the books seems appropriate. Communities go into economic development programs for reasons ranging from the compelling to the trivial—from an urgent need for jobs to an underemployed and impoverished population to the perception, by the political powers that be, that an economic development program looks good politically, generates lots of publicity, won't cost very much, and can't do any harm. The time for thinking about whether a program is needed and, if it is, what basic direction it should take is before the program is started. For once the program begins, both the pressure of work and the political momentum of the program will crowd out serious reflection. The writer has tried to suggest the questions which every community should consider before embarking on the voyage.

CONTENTS

ECONOMIC DEVELOPMENT PROGRAMS FOR CITIES, COUNTIES, AND TOWNS

1

INTRODUCTION

There are about 15,000 organizations in the United States devoted to the promotion of local economic growth, and their number appears to be increasing rapidly.[1] They appear in a bewildering variety of forms—among others, governmental and quasi-governmental agencies, nonprofit corporations, local development corporations. They range in size from chambers of commerce, with minimal budgets and no paid staff, to development corporations with large staffs and multimillion-dollar budgets.

Though no precise figures exist on the subject, it is clear that some billions of dollars per year are expended nationally on local economic development. These expenditures include the cost of operating the multitude of development organizations: a wide variety of direct subsidies given to industry by local, state, and national government; and an equally wide variety of tax outlays, ranging from local property-tax abatement to very substantial tax forgiveness, by IRS on tax-exempt financings.

Local economic development is an intensely competitive activity. Whether the development agency is striving to bring in a firm, to prevent the departure of a firm, or to encourage an expansion, it is in competition with a very large number of rivals. Whether it is the competition to attract firms, or the competition between communities for a limited amount of development funding (generally from the federal government), the economic developer exists in a world just as competitive as that of the firms which are his quarry—and sometimes more so.

If economic development is a goal so earnestly pursued by so many communities, it may seem odd for a book on economic development to begin with the question, "Is a development program needed?" Nevertheless, it is a question which any community considering a program should ponder, and a logical point at which to begin a book on economic development. Economic development offers many benefits to communities. Inevitably, it wil exact some price. There are many valid and praiseworthy reasons for pursuing an active development policy. But there are also many not-so-valid and not-so-praiseworthy reasons for doing so.

ECONOMIC DEVELOPMENT AND UNEMPLOYMENT

Perhaps the most common, and certainly the most readily justified reason for a local economic development program is the need to create jobs both to reduce unemployment and to exert upward pressure on wages. The progenitor of modern local economic development programs originated in Mississippi during the Great Depression.[2] Named BAWI (Balance Agriculture with Industry), its goal was to provide manufacturing jobs for a desperately poor and often unemployed rural and small-town population. Today, the two federal agencies most heavily involved in providing direct financial assistance to promote local economic development make poverty and unemployment primary criteria for determining eligibility for funding.

The justification for local economic development as a cure for unemployment and poverty rests upon one central fact: People are less mobile than capital. Were people as mobile as capital, the loss of an industry would be followed by an outmigration of workers and their dependents, preventing the unemployment rate from rising and preventing the wage rate from falling. Conversely, the opening of a new industry would draw in enough new workers to prevent the unemployment rate from falling and to prevent wage rates from rising. In terms of labor markets, it would not be possible to justify local economic development programs.

But perfect mobility is not the case. The population adjusts only slowly to economic change. Nationally, the shift from coal to oil occurred in the 1940s, yet the population which had built up in parts of Kentucky, Ohio, West Virginia, and other eastern coal areas has largely remained in place to the present time, with persisting low wage levels and high unemployment rates. Perhaps the increasing demand for coal, in the face of rising petroleum prices, will reverse the economic fortunes of many of these areas. If so, it will be a matter of jobs coming to people, and not the reverse.

A similar immobility of labor in the face of job shifts is seen in urban areas. From 1969 through 1975, New York City lost an incredible total of half a million jobs. Yet city population shrank only slightly. The job loss manifested itself more in increased unemployment, decreased labor-force participation, and increased public assistance than it did in outmigration of population.

When population does decline as a result of job losses, the decline is not generally an across-the-board one. Numerous studies show that those most prone to leave an economically declining area are younger adults with above-average incomes and above-average education. To a lesser degree, there is a loss of children in the population simply because it is young adults who have young children. Age, poverty, and lack of education are all predispositions to immo-bility. This is hardly surprising, for it seems only reasonable that youth, education, and money should give people the energy and confidence to pull up stakes and move. Thus, declining areas often lose precisely the people they can least afford to lose.

Although detailed discussion of labor markets is put off until Chapter 11, let us consider some major indications that the local job market may be inade-quate for the population it serves.

High Unemployment and Low Labor-Force Participation Rates

The unemployment rate is probably the most widely cited economic statis-tic in the United States. Obviously, persistently high rates are an indication of a mismatch between economic base and population and are the single strongest reason for implementing a development program.

Persistent unemployment causes people to drop out of the labor force. The prospects for finding work may become so dim that potential workers simply stop looking. At that point they cease to be counted as unemployed. Thus, as useful as the unemployment rate may be, it does not present a full picture of the labor market. Low participation rates are an indication of the presence of discouraged workers, and signal that labor-market conditions may well be worse than the unemployment rate indicates. Participation rates by age, sex, and race provide an insight into labor-market conditions that the unemploy-ment rate alone does not give. These insights can be very useful in program design.

For example, a normal male participation rate, combined with a very low female participation rate, might suggest a development program targeted at bringing in or developing light-assembly or office activities that would be ex-pected to provide a high percentage of jobs for women. A higher-than-average labor-force participation rate for women, accompanied by a lower-than-average rate for men, might suggest an economy which provides an adequate number of service, clerical, and domestic jobs, but which is in need of more blue-collar and industrial opportunities. (In fact, the higher-than-average female participation/ lower-than-average male participation rate often characterizes urban black popu-lations, and results partly from the fact that clerical and domestic employment is more readily available for women than is manufacturing and other blue-collar employment for men.)

Cyclical Instability

Unemployment-rate fluctuations above the national average are an indica-tion that an area is specialized in characteristically unstable industries. Typically, though not universally, an industrial base heavily oriented toward capital goods and durable-goods manufacturing, or heavily dependent on government contracts tends toward large cyclical swings. A history of cyclical instability may argue for an economic development program that emphasizes diversification or that seeks to bring in industries noted for relative constancy of demand (much nondurable-goods manufacturing falls in this category, as do many service activities).

Low Levels of Personal or Family Income

Average wages may be low because an area has more than its share of low-wage industries, or because its industries pay lower wages than do their counterparts in other labor markets. The symptoms thus may be similar while the diseases are quite different. Family incomes may be low because of low wage rates or low participation rates. Two industrial areas that pay similar wages to male workers may exhibit very different family-income statistics if one offers numerous jobs for women, while another does not. To the extent that the problem is understood, a development program can be designed to deal with it.

A development program which brings jobs into an area—whether by attracting new firms or encouraging present firms to expand—offers the prospect of tightening the labor market, with the effect of driving down the unemployment rate, pushing up participation rates, and elevating wages as the competition among firms for workers increases. Ideally, the program should be targeted at bringing in the types of jobs most needed. Even if a program's retention and recruitment activities cannot be given a precise target—as is very often the case—almost any increase in jobs will have some tightening effects.

But here, a caveat is important: People are much more mobile in the face of job opportunities than in the face of job losses. If a factory in a small town closes and 100 jobs are lost, the number of residents who move out may be extremely small. The job loss will manifest itself through some increase in unemployment and some decrease in participation rates. Some people who were dual job holders may become single job holders. On the other hand, should a new factory open in a comparable small town, a very considerable number of people may come in to take the new jobs. The decrease in unemployment and the increase in participation rates among the original population may thus be far smaller than a naïve estimate would have indicated. This point is discussed in more detail in Chapter 12.

Writing about labor markets in southern towns that are now gaining industry at a rapid pace, one writer notes:

> Relocating manufacturers contend that they do not have to depend on workers already in town. They simply announce in, say, the Baltimore newspapers that they are headed for, say, Lynchburg, and the native sons return with Northern-acquired skills. In almost any

Southern town from which blue-collar workers have migrated, some reluctantly, many have tired of the big city and would like to return, but they need a good job. When a new plant comes in, they come back. In fact, the hard corollary to this easy mobility is that local growth does not really lick the unemployment problem—all it does, in the long run, is enlarge the local labor force. Since it is the returning skilled workers who win away most of the new jobs, the town just gets bigger, still struggling with its chronic unemployment problem—its 'unemployables.'[3]

It is hardly surprising that the gaining of jobs is far more likely to encourage inmigration than is the loss of jobs likely to encourage immediate outmigration. It takes far less courage to move to a new job than it does to move into a new area with no guarantee of employment.

ECONOMIC DEVELOPMENT AND PROPERTY TAXES

In recent years, what might be regarded as a somewhat less legitimate reason for mounting economic development programs has come to the fore: property tax relief. Increasing costs of local government and increasing citizen resistance to rising local taxes—particularly the property tax—have put many local governments in an uncomfortable fiscal position. In some cases, the difficulty is compounded by constitutional limits on either bonded indebtedness or on tax rate as a percentage of the value of taxable real property. For the community in a fiscal bind, whatever the cause, bringing in new commercial ratables that promise to yield far more in revenues than they will demand in services is an obvious solution to the problem.

The emphasis on economic development as a property tax relief program, rather than a jobs program, is particularly common where the community is small relative to its labor market. The reason is quite simple. Where jurisdictions are small relative to the metropolitan area, what any one community can do to affect its own labor market is minimal. Most of its residents do not work in that community and most workers in that community are not residents. However, if a new commercial facility can be brought in, all of the property taxes it pays accrue to the treasury of that municipality. Thus in many suburban areas, there is intense competition among relatively prosperous communities motivated almost entirely by fiscal rather than labor-market considerations. The success of a development program is judged far more on the basis of the taxable value of new facilities than on the number of jobs they offer. In fact, the provision of jobs may be regarded only as an unpleasant side effect that must be accepted in order to get the ratable.

While the reader—as does the writer—may regard the easing of the property-tax burden as a generally less compelling reason than labor-market conditions for local economic development programs, there is no gainsaying the fact that many such programs have primarily fiscal motivations.

Other Motivations for Local Economic Development Programs

Another common motivation behind the promotion of economic growth is simply the fact that growth is often good for the established business community. As economic growth increases the demand for goods, services, and property, merchants, local service businesses, and property owners benefit. Retailers benefit through increased sales, and property owners, both business and residential, benefit through higher rents and lower vacancy rates. The legitimacy of this last reason is a matter for the reader to contemplate.

Because economic development appears to offer something for so many diverse elements in the community—jobs for unemployed workers, increased sales for retailers, capital gains for property owners, increased loan business for local banks, higher rents for apartment owners, increased commissions for the local real estate brokerage industry—the economic developer often puts together a constituency of rather diverse elements. Union leaders and businessmen, wealthy property owners, and minority advocates, if able to agree on little else, can agree on the need for economic growth. Like politics, economic development makes strange bedfellows.

The Side Effects of Economic Development

If economic development programs offer improved labor-market conditions (from the workers' viewpoint), property-tax relief, and higher profits for many segments of the business community, are there cases in which public encouragement of economic growth is inadvisable?

A successful economic growth program will, inevitably, have side effects. Whether these are serious enough to argue against beginning a program is a matter to be determined case by case. But it is important to recognize these effects and anticipate them, rather than to discover them later.

Housing-Market Effects

Much of the demand for housing comes from the availability of jobs. Economic growth tightens housing markets. Prices and rents go up and vacancy rates go down. How much the market is tightened by economic growth will depend on many factors. One, obviously, is the amount of growth relative to the size of the housing market in which new workers must find shelter. Another, perhaps slightly less obvious factor, is the elasticity of the housing stock. Can the housing stock expand readily? Or are there physical or legal factors that constrain expansion of the housing stock? A given amount of economic growth in San Francisco, where there is little unbuilt land in the city, and where steep topography limits growth outside the city, may produce considerable pressure on real estate markets. A comparable amount of growth in Des Moines or Indianapolis, where there are not comparable obstacles to the expansion of the housing stock, may produce much smaller effects.

In many suburban areas, barriers to the expansion of the housing stock may be legal rather than physical. Where a policy of encouraging economic growth is combined with land-use controls that limit residential construction, the housing-market effects of economic growth may be extremely powerful. For instance, in southern Fairfield County, Connecticut, a house which can be bought for less than six figures is a rarity. Unquestionably, one reason for this level of real estate prices, which would be regarded as spectacular in most of the United States, is that massive economic growth has occurred in an area in which rigid land-use controls severely limit the construction of housing. A similar phenomenon can be seen in and around Washington, D.C.

For the worker who benefits directly from economic growth, or for the family which is converted from a one- to a two-income family because of new employment opportunities, the higher housing costs may be a minor price to pay for newfound prosperity. For the property owner, the higher level of prices may be a much appreciated windfall. But for the retired person, or for anyone who is not a beneficiary of the tightened labor market, the higher price and rent levels may be a considerable burden. Wilbur Thompson notes: "It is irresponsible to promote local industrial expansion without coupling this action to a low income housing policy that picks up the pieces. But we do it all the time."[4] While that is a far stronger and more categorical statement than this writer would care to make, the fact is that there is a nexus between housing markets and job markets that ought to be thought about before embarking on a development program.

Environmental Effects

Environmental effects are more generally recognized than housing-market effects. Very evidently, all economic development has some environmental impact. For most activities other than power generation, materials processing, and some heavy industry, the most serious environmental effect is likely to stem from automotive emissions. Nonetheless, the effect is there and a community price must be paid. Often, the economic developer will find himself at odds with local environmental movements. More will be said about this later, but he is often well advised to bring the environmental movement into the development-planning process early, rather than confronting it later in the media or the courts.

Social Stress, and Political and Fiscal Change

In general, economic growth promotes inmigration. Demographic change—both in terms of structure of population and just size of population—will place some stress on the existing social fabric. The effects of inmigration may produce changes which are ultimately seen by most as beneficial, or inmigration resulting from development may prove traumatic, with massive increases in crime, alcoholism, prostitution. Again it is hard to generalize. The opening of a think tank in suburbia and the initiation of a massive construction project in a small, isolated town both qualify as economic development, but they have little else in common.

To the extent that the incoming population is different from the in-place population in habits, values, and attitudes, economic growth promotes political change. This is not to say that such change is bad, but merely that it should be considered.

Economic development, as noted, is often advocated to relieve fiscal pressures. And, indeed, it often does. Yet it is also possible for the inmigration fostered by industrial or commercial development to make demands upon a municipality that cost more to satisfy than the new plant and the new residents contribute in revenues. If the increase in population pushes a municipality into major expansions of sewer and water systems, major construction of schools, and the provision of urban services not previously offered, the result may actually be a net fiscal loss. Occasionally, a seeming paradox occurs in which the newcomers pay more than their share of taxes and yet taxes still go up. If the incoming population has fundamentally different expectations of public services, it may change the case of a once sleepy municipality from a low-tax/low-services situation to a high-tax/high-services situation. The result may be quite painful to some members of the original population. The oldtimers will resent the new levels of expenditure, while the newcomers may feel entirely righteous because they are carrying their full share of the tax burden. This situation has been observed in suburban communities when the inmigrating population has been substantially wealthier than the native population. But there is no reason to believe it is confined to suburban areas.

None of the above side effects are cited as admonitions against economic development. The writer's experience, and what survey data are available, indicate that communities are, more often than not, pleased with the results of development programs. Rather, the effects are cited because they should be given serious consideration. Economic development will exact some prices, and these should be acknowledged and considered before deciding whether or not to embark upon a program. If the decision is to go ahead, then recognition of the side effects may make it possible to deal with them more effectively.

NOTES

1. No hard numbers are available. A figure of 14,000 to 17,000 is cited commonly, but its origin is obscure. At present, it appears that growth in the field is more rapid on the public than on the private side. As a very coarse indication of growth, a comparable figure of 7,000 to 10,000 was cited a decade ago. See Ted Levine, "Attracting Industry: The Use and Abuse of Advertising and Promotion," in *Guide to Industrial Development*, Dick Howard, ed., Prentice-Hall, Englewood Cliffs, N.J., 1972.

2. For a history of early local development efforts, see Alfred Eichner, *Development Agencies and Employment Expansion*, Wayne State University Press, Detroit, 1970.

3. Wilbur Thompson, "Economic Processes and Employment Problems in Declining Metropolitan Areas," in *Post-Industrial America: Metropolitan Decline and Inter-Regional Job Shifts*, George Sternlieb and James W. Hughes, eds., State University of New Jersey, Center for Urban Policy Research, Rutgers, New Brunswick, 1975.

4. Wilbur Thompson, "Problems that Sprout in the Shadow of No-Growth," *AIA Journal*, December 1973.

2

THE POLITICAL CONTEXT
OF ECONOMIC DEVELOPMENT

In general, economic development programs have a very high degree of political visibility. A two-person economic development agency is likely to generate more press and media coverage than a much larger public-works department. Economic development activity is essentially newsworthy so far as local media are concerned. Plant openings and closings, promotional campaigns, the relationship between tax ratables and the property-tax rate—these are of continuing interest to local residents. Not only is economic development activity newsworthy, but for reasons discussed in Chapter 8, media exposure is generally to be sought, not shunned.

Development agencies are often quite useful politically, and this fact is often one reason why they are created. Development programs are popular. Liberals and conservatives may disagree about how much to tax, who to tax, and what to spend on. But they are likely to agree on a program which promises jobs to the working man and relief to the property owner.

The connection between the clamor for property-tax relief and the popularity of economic development is an obvious one. Beyond that, in a period in which the public's esteem for government, relative to private industry, is sinking, economic development programs may enable government to borrow a certain prestige. Rather than appearing as taxer and spender, government appears as a facilitator of beneficial private development. To the suffering taxpayer, government appears a friend rather than foe. Economic development is one government activity which is popular in a period of increasing conservatism. CETA, a federally funded job-training and -creation program, has come in for an enormous amount of criticism on the grounds of waste, incompetence, and inefficiency. Total government spending for local economic development, which may be roughly comparable to CETA in amount, if one combines a variety of direct-grant and indirect-subsidy (tax-expenditure) programs, has been subject to very little criticism.[1]

The fact that local economic development activities are highly visible and often politically useful also makes them lightning rods for criticism. If the incumbent mayor or county executive has created an economic development organization a year ago, his political opponent can criticize him because the organization he is funding out of the taxpayers' hard-earned money has yet to sign a single contract or bring in a single firm. If a firm moves out of the area, it can belabor him with charges that he and his development agency should have prevented this.

The incumbent may reply, in perfect truth, that economic development is a slow and uncertain process and that his opponent's expectations are unreasonable. He may note that in any large area, firms are always moving in both directions. He may also note that the power of local government to influence the behavior of any single firm is limited. But the fact is that any economic development program, other than a long-established one with an unarguable track record, is prone to such attack.

Most development agencies operate under pressure to show results. This is particularly true in the first few years of operation. There can be no arguing that a city must have a police department, a fire department, a sanitation department. Not only is the need for these departments generally agreed upon, but what they do and when they do it is usually clear. The same cannot be said regarding economic development agencies. They are not necessities in the same sense as fire departments. Nor is it quite so clear what they do. They produce their results erratically, intermittently, and sometimes with long spaces in between.

Furthermore, it is not always possible to say exactly what they have accomplished. By the time a firm moves into an area, its officers have probably had contacts with local brokers, bankers, planning and zoning officials, public officials, other businessmen, and various others. In a sense, bringing in the company has been a collective effort, and it is hard to determine exactly what role any single party has played. If the development agency has arranged for a subsidy or tax abatement, there may be some question as to whether the firm would have moved in without the inducement.

One result of this pressure is a tendency for the new agency, or the agency which has not completed a deal in some time, to become unselective and to involve itself in arrangements and efforts against its better judgment. Similarly, there is often much pressure for premature disclosure. The desire to look good and to show results may encourage an agency to represent a possible or probable deal as a fait accompli. To the extent that negotiations may be upset by premature publicity, or that claiming credit for an event which subsequently does not take place may destroy agency credibility, this pressure should be resisted. That is not always easy to do. This is particularly so when pressure comes from the political structure which has created the development agency and selected its personnel. Keeping a promising but not-quite-jelled deal under wraps, in the face of an impending election, for example, may be advisable but also very difficult.

Economic development is a highly competitive activity. Intermunicipality as well as interstate and interregional competition for new firms is intense. The firm known to be contemplating a move, or even the firm which simply looks as though it would be a good addition to the local economy and tax base, is often besieged by suitors. Many firms become quite sophisticated about using offers from one agency to motivate other agencies, adding to the economic developer's sense of competition. Even the economic developer who sees his main function as that of retaining and developing existing industry will feel competition from the recruiting efforts of other agencies.

The field is often competitive in still another sense. In larger cities and counties, there are usually a number of agencies involved in economic development. For example, in a large county containing a number of towns or cities, there may be competition between levels of government. Within the same jurisdiction, there may be competition between governmental and nongovernmental organizations. In some cases there may be competition between different agencies in the same governmenmental structure. Very often a mixture of competition and cooperation may prevail. A local chamber of commerce and a governmental development agency may cooperate on recruiting a firm and then compete to see who gets public credit. The writer witnessed one instance in which a state and a county development agency cooperated splendidly in bringing in and arranging financing for a firm, and then exchanged rather harsh words afterward when one sent out a press release without consulting the other. The acrimony was founded not in childishness, but in the accurate perception that appearances have a bearing on both agency effectiveness and continuity of employment for agency personnel.

Another aspect of the political setting of economic development is the fact that economic development, as a profession, has no fixed set of credentials or licensing procedure.[2] The public-works commissioner may be required to have a professional engineer's license, and the planning commissioner may be required to have a master's degree in planning or certification from the American Planning Association. But no comparable requirements are likely to exist for the director of economic development. This situation, combined with the fact that economic development activity provides the practitioner with a high degree of public visibility and an opportunity to become well known, may make the economic development organization a source of jobs with which to reward campaign workers and other political loyalists. While there are a large number of highly competent people engaged in the practice of economic development, it must be said that the politicization of the field also results in the presence of many practitioners whose education and past experience do not appear to be suited to it (though some may do quite well once they get into it).

Because of its close links to politics in the several ways previously discussed, economic development, as a profession, does not offer a great deal of stability. The head of an association of economic development agencies told the author, "Ten years ago I knew the head of the economic development agency in every major U.S. city. Today, most of them are still active in economic development, but not one is in the same job." The work offers variety, public exposure, and a chance to be well known within a community. If one's efforts are successful, it offers considerable feelings of accomplishment. Often it pays well. But it is not a good choice for those who have particularly strong needs for security and stability.

THE DEVELOPMENT COALITION

One task for the recently formed development agancy is building a coalition in favor of development. The economic developer who constructs such a coalition is more likely to be effective and will be better insulated against the vagaries of politics.

In most communities the essentials of a coalition for development are present and waiting for the economic developer. Property owners, in general, are likely to be for development because it holds out prospects for reduced tax burdens. Those who own property whose market value will rise as development increases demand have a second reason to favor development. This may be equally true of the owners of vacant land with commercial potential, of owners of stores and commercial buildings, and of apartment owners. Homeowners may perceive that economic growth increases the demand for housing, and that therefore they will ultimately profit from it. In the writer's experience, most businessmen are in favor of growth even when it does not serve their narrow interests. A local manufacturer, for example, is likely to favor economic development as a matter of principle even though it may tighten labor markets and increase his wage costs. The banking community is generally for development since it means more loan business. Commercial realtors are almost invariably for development for similar reasons. However, one must note here that their generally favorable development position may be tempered by fears that an active development agency may from time to time connect a buyer with a property owner directly, thus causing a broker to lose a commission.

Organized labor is almost inevitably for development and can be a major piece in the coalition for development. The only caution here is that the economic developer should ask himself whether the face his labor people will present to potential employers is one of cooperation and accommodation, or one of rigidity and hard-nosed militancy. If it is the former, they will be valuable allies; if it is the latter, their support is more to be desired from a distance than from close in.

Particularly in the early stages of a development agency's life, time spent acquainting these various constituencies with the agency's purposes and personnel is time well spent, even though it may show no immediate results. This matter is discussed in greater length in Chaper 8.

In most communities, economic development will have some opponents, and it is well not to ignore them. Economic growth promotes change—physical, social, political. Some opposition to economic development will thus spring from this root. Opposition to economic development may come from expectations of increased traffic or increased population. In the suburban rings around major cities, economic development may be opposed because it brings with it the specter of urbanization. If the suburb is largely peopled by those who have come to it recently to escape the real or imagined evils of urban life, opposition on this count may be very strong.

In recent years, environmental consciousness has grown and with it, the strength of the environmental movement. This is true both in terms of political power and statutory authority. The general clash between the claims of environmental quality and economic need are by now well known. Much opposition to economic development will come from local environmental groups. Such opposition can be quite formidable. Local environmental groups often have a generally upper-middle-class membership that is politically well connected and articulate. Then, too, environmental groups often have a certain moral aura about them. Finally, environmental law is now sufficiently complex that litigation may delay a project for years, if not decades.

Where jurisdictions are small, opposition based on either planning or environmental issues may be particularly strong. This is because most of the benefit in terms of increased employment will accrue to people who live outside the municipality, whereas much of the traffic and environmental impact will occur within the municipality. Thus, many of those who would be for the project, but relatively few who are opposed, are politically disenfranchised.

The agency run by the writer several years ago attempted to finance the development of a light-manufacturing firm in a municipality with an area of about two square miles. The municipality is part of the New York region, which, in less than a decade, had lost half a million manufacturing jobs. To the author and his agency, the virtue of the project seemed unarguable. Nonetheless, the agency ultimately had to back off and drop the project as a result of determined and skillfully organized citizen opposition. Opponents of the project pointed out that few of the firm's workers would live in the community, and that, furthermore, few of the plant's workers would have the income to even contemplate buying a house in this predominantly middle- and upper-middle class community. Few gains for local retailers were seen, for as one citizen opponent noted of the plant's presumed labor force, "Those are the kind of people who bring their lunch to work in a paper bag." Thus, community gains from the project seemed small, and what the author perceived as the regionwide gains carried little weight with community residents.

If opposition to economic development is likely to come from planning and environmental constituencies, what is the economic developer to do? In some cases, where there are uncompromisable differences between the goals of different groups, the matter will come down to a test of political strength or to judicial decision.

Nonetheless, the economic development agency may be able to minimize conflict and opposition by involving members of the potential opposition early on in the economic development process. For example, assume a citizen advisory board for an economic development agency is to be set up. One member of the board might be a prominent figure in the local environmental movement. This serves several purposes. First, it serves a mutual education function. The environmentalist on the board is exposed to the goals of the program and the needs which the program seeks to meet. In due time, this exposure may create some rapport. If the environmentalist, for example, is a member of the upper middle class who has few blue-collar contacts, sitting next to a labor union leader may make him or her more sympathetic to the need for blue-collar jobs. Conversely, having an environmentalist on the board may make the board more conscious of the concerns of the environmental movement and of the real environmental costs of some projects. If a proposed project has serious environmental flaws, perhaps there may be room for some compromise and redesign. If potential conflicts can be discovered early, they can be discussed quietly, calmly, and privately at an early stage in the process. The chances of a mutually acceptable solution are far greater than if the same issues are aired late in the process in a public and highly political forum.

Similarly, there is a certain wisdom for including one or more representatives of what might be considered the planning or general public-interest constituency in the development coalition. Again the goal is partly mutual education and partly early recognition of potential conflict. At one time, the writer was responsible for proposing the membership of the five-person board of a development financing agency. For one seat, he proposed a member of the planning establishment. The seat was filled by the chairman of the county planning board, an arrangement which worked very smoothly. Planning concerns were represented and, at the same time, the agency received some protection from charges that it was oblivious to the cause of good planning.

Apart from bringing members of the potential opposition into the process in a formal way, there is much to be said for informal communication. Ideally, this should begin before there is a specific bone of contention. In the early stages of an agency's existence, its personnel might hold conversations with environmentalists, planners, and representatives of such groups as the League of Women Voters, explaining the agency's goals and exploring areas of common interest and potential conflict. Such conversations open up a dialogue and avoid feelings of being ignored or of being surprised. Surprise is desirable for birthdays and anniversaries, but in the political world its most likely products are anger and opposition.

Obviously, the economic developer must scrupulously respect the confidences of firms, property owners, brokers, and others with whom he has dealings. If he does not, his credibility will soon be gone and his capacity to do useful work destroyed. At the same time, to the extent that the potential opposition can be taken into the economic developer's confidence and included in the development process, opposition may be minimized and compromise furthered.

NOTES

1. One exception to this statement is found in "Bidding for Business," Public Interest Research Group, Washington, D.C., 1979. Published by a group under the Ralph Nader aegis, this booklet is, as might be expected, highly critical of public expenditures which subsidize private economic development.

2. The American Industrial Development Council (AIDC), located in Kansas City, Mo., does give courses for industrial developers and issues a designation as a certified industrial developer (CID) to practitioners, on the basis of experience and an examination.

3

WHAT DEVELOPMENT AGENCIES DO

Although agencies vary tremendously by size and type and, to a lesser degree, by purpose, there is a core of activity common to most. Agency functions can be grouped into a few main categories:

- public relations, advertising, marketing, and provision of information
- ombudsman and liaison functions
- financing assistance
- tax abatement
- development planning
- the use of public and other legal powers to facilitate development

Though not every agency engages in all of the above, there are few functions performed by development agencies that cannot readily be fitted into one or more of the above categories.

PUBLIC RELATIONS, ADVERTISING, AND MARKETING

Economists often talk about a "perfect market," one of whose characteristics is that both buyers and sellers are fully informed of all possibilities. All buyers are aware of everything which is for sale in the market and the asking price. Conversely, sellers are aware of every offering price.

Were the market for commercial sites, commercial structures, and economic locations a perfect market, the role of the economic developer would be far smaller and simpler than it is, and the need for his services greatly reduced.

17

The most central fact about the markets with which the industrial developer is concerned is that they are very far from perfect. Because of this imperfection, public relations, advertising, and promotion justifiably take up more of the industrial developer's time than any other category of activity. In many cases, they may take up more of his time than all other activities combined.

Consider the matter from the point of view of a firm determined to find a location within a given area, say, the state of Pennsylvania. For the firm to narrow its decision down to a single county in a rational manner would require the acquisition of a formidable amount of information, which is not available from any central source. Among the items needed would be land costs, construction costs, property-tax rates, other tax rates, utility costs, labor-force availability, wage rates, financial inducements and tax abatements, transportation facilities, land-use controls, environmental regulations. Putting together such an information package is time consuming and expensive. Nor would it be the end of the decision process. Though one might gather information on typical site or typical building costs, the fact is that there are no absolutely typical sites or typical buildings. There are only particular sites and particular buildings. Though there are average property-tax rates, one does not pay average taxes. One pays taxes on particular properties. And so on.

The gathering of locational information is difficult and expensive. All locational decisions are made, to some degree, on the basis of less-than-complete information. The municipality which makes itself and its advantages known has an edge over the municipality which has equal assets but which does not make them known.

The locational decisions—whether it is the decision to stay, to move, to expand in place, or to branch out—are not made casually. Locations for business activity are not chosen with the casualness that consumer goods may be chosen. The economic developer might take it as a general rule that he cannot sell his community to a firm for which that community is wrong. On the other hand, there is much to be gained from reaching firms for which the community may be right.

Thus, most development agencies advertise. Advertising never sells the community by itself, but it opens a dialogue between the firm and the economic developer. Most economic development agencies engage in public-relations activities to make both their locality and their own existence known. This may take the form of media exposure, of public appearances, or of events. Its function, like that of paid advertising, is to create interest in the community as an economic location and to begin a dialogue between the economic developer and the potential firm.

A major function of economic development agencies, beyond that of bringing in new businesses, is that of retaining existing businesses. Very often a development agency can forestall a move out by remedying a problem or offering an incentive. More than one threatened move out has been converted into an expansion in place by financing assistance or tax abatement. In some cases a move out may be forestalled by some simple action, such as expediting the granting of a permit. But for the economic developer to have the opportunity to do these things, he must have contact with the firm. The visibility that an agency's public-relations effort gives it is a key to having the necessary contact.

Most development agencies initiate direct contact with firms as well as responding to firms which seek them out. If the main role of the agency is retention of existing industry, most of these contacts may be with firms in the area. If the agency sees its main role as bringing in firms, most of its contacts may be with firms outside the area. Contact may be made by letter, by phone, by personal visit, through intermediaries, or through participation in trade shows and conventions. Again, the purpose is to begin a dialogue to see whether there is a mutuality of interest between the firm and the community.

The gathering of information is (as noted above) time consuming and expensive from the firm's point of view. Thus the community that can provide a mass of useful information has a major advantage over its competitor which does not. Most development agencies attempt to develop a data base on the community they represent. Such an effort can be laborious, but it is usually worth doing. It is a natural followup to the advertising, public-relations, and promotional effort. In fact, a public-relations and advertising effort that is not backed by a solid body of information is likely to do more harm than good. It builds up expectations which cannot be met, creates an impression of lack of seriousness, and ends by creating frustration and irritation.

Ombudsman and Liaison Functions

In spite of the fact that local government may be eager to attract and retain industry, its own actions—or inactions—may drive industry out. One function of the economic developer is to act as an intermediary and reduce this effect as much as possible. In some cases, of course, there is genuine conflict between the needs or wants of industry and legitimate community goals and needs. But in many cases, there is no real conflict of interests; rather, there are merely procedural or formal problems. In some cases, the economic developer may be able to help by simply getting the local bureaucracy to move more expeditiously. A firm may have difficulties with a local zoning board, not over a matter of real substance, but over minor matters of form and technicality. The economic developer, through the use of his good offices, may be able to resolve such questions. Very often, those on the public side of the fence are not conscious of the extent to which time is money to entrepreneurs. For a builder with a $10 million construction loan at 15 percent, a one-day delay costs over $4,000 in debt service alone. The economic developer may perform a very useful service by simply making things happen just a little more quickly.

FINANCING ASSISTANCE

A very large amount of financing assistance is now available to business and industry for the purpose of influencing locational decisions. Whether the total sum of industrial and commercial development in the United States is significantly influenced by the existence of this variety of direct and indirect subsidies is a matter of some debate. There is little doubt, however, that in the competition between places, whether they be cities, counties, development districts, or states, the ability to offer financing assistance is an important consideration. Its importance grows as the other differences between places diminish. Thus, a firm is not likely to decide between locating in the Northeast or the Southwest primarily on the basis of financing assistance. But once having made a choice of region, the choice of a particular place may be very heavily influenced by the availability of financing assistance. Financing assistance takes several general forms. Most agencies pursue federal grants for economic development. The two most common sources of federal grant assistance are the Economic Development Administration (EDA) and the Department of Housing and Urban Development (HUD). In 47 of the 50 states, development agencies may issue tax-exempt financing to promote economic development. A great many development agencies are involved in this process, which offers firms quite substantial reductions in debt-service costs and can be almost costless to the issuing agency.

Most agencies are also involved in guiding firms to a variety of financing-assistance sources. These may include venture-capital corporations, such federal agencies as the Small Business Administration, small-business investment corporations, and other sources. They generally also include a variety of state programs. For the entrepreneur relatively unfamiliar with the workings of government, learning what is available can be a difficult process. The development agency may perform a valuable service by guiding the firm through what appears to be an impenetrable bureaucratic and administrative forest. This is particularly so for small firms with limited staff resources.

Finally, many agencies expend funds directly on behalf of firms. This may take the form of loans, grants, writedowns. Regardless of whether the development agency is merely a guide and conduit to sources of financial assistance, or whether the agency is actually itself a source of assistance, financial assistance to encourage development is a key function of almost any development agency.

Tax Abatement

A very large percentage of all political jurisdictions in the United States offer some form of tax abatement to encourage industrial and commercial development. Abatements of local property taxes and state corporate-income taxes are the most commonly offered abatements below the federal level. While abatements are offered by the taxing jurisdiction itself, guiding firms to these abatements, helping firms apply for them, and, in some cases, helping to design and enact the abatements in the first instance are important agency functions.

DEVELOPMENT PLANNING

Physical planning efforts by development agencies vary tremendously. Ideally, in an area in which significant development is desired and expected, planning efforts and economic development efforts are integrated. Obviously, economic development has planning implications in terms of land use, traffic flows, housing, demands upon public facilities. Conversely, many of the questions with which planners are concerned have economic development implications. In suburban areas, for example, the largest single determinant of the location of economic activity is highway access. The spacing of interchanges on a limited-access highway, for example, is often critical in determining where activity will locate. Land-use controls judiciously applied may promote and guide development very successfully, while land-use controls badly applied may block development or produce undesirable development. The use of the community's capital budget—particularly for transportation facilities and public utilities—is a key instrument in shaping and promoting economic development. The community seriously interested in major economic development is thus well advised to integrate its economic development, land-use planning, and capital-budgeting processes. In recent years, with the growth of environmental concerns and legal requirements, municipalities may also be well advised to integrate environmental planning with economic development planning. It is far better to resolve conflicts, between environmental and economic development goals, internally and early on than later on in acrimonious public debate or litigation.

Going down one step from the completely integrated planning effort, many agencies plan at what might be called the public-entrepreneurial level. That is, the agency develops projects and then acts as financier and marketer. The agency, for example, may assemble land, absorb part of that cost, and then sell or lease sites to firms. Agencies frequently build facilities for lease to firms.

In many other instances, development agencies do little or no physical planning. For example, a development agency in a developed and now stagnant urban area may largely occupy itself with attempting to retain existing industry. Its recruitment efforts may be devoted to bringing new industry into existing buildings or to encouraging new industry to build on vacant parcels within an existing street and utility pattern. For example, the New York City Industrial Development Agency, which is essentially a development-financing agency, has done yeoman service for the city in retaining and financing the expansion of firms within the city. It is, clearly, a successful effort. But it is not heavily involved in development planning. Its mission is one of preserving an existing structure, not of creating a new structure.

The writer, at one time, operated a suburban economic development agency whose primary functions were promotion and financing. While the agency considered established planning goals and would not finance development which violated these goals, it did not plan in the sense that the term is normally used by land-use planners. It did, from time to time, take positions or otherwise contribute to legislative and capital-budget questions where these had economic development implications.

The Use of Public and Other Powers

Where the development agency is not a part of government—though it may be the legal creation of government—it often exercises governmental or quasi-governmental powers. In some cases, agencies may have powers which are denied government by constitutional limitations and may thus be able to act for the public benefit in ways that government may not. For example, a number of state constitutions have provisions which prohibit gifts and loans by the state to individuals or corporations. A development agency may thus be able to subsidize development in ways that government may not. Development agencies may also be vested with powers which are common to governments. Thus, a development agency may have a power of condemnation that it can use in the process of land assembly. Many development agencies have the power to issue tax-exempt funding, a power normally reserved for units of government. The agency may also have powers normal for both business and government—for example, the power to enter into contracts, the power to sue or be sued, the power to appoint officers and adopt bylaws. The exercise of these powers in the pursuit of development goals is thus one of its functions.

4

AGENCY TYPE AND STRUCTURE

    Development organizations vary tremendously in internal structure and in position within the political structure. Because political and economic environments vary so much, it is not possible to assert that one organizational form is superior to others. This chapter sketches various types and structures, and notes some of the factors to be considered in setting up a development organization.

    Development agencies might be loosely divided into the following categories:

• Public agencies: these are agencies which are legally and administratively part of the structure of government. They may be line agencies, component parts of line agencies, or staff agencies. An example of the first type would be a separate department of economic development. An example of the second would be an economic development office included in a planning, community development, or public-works department. An example of the third type might be an office of economic development, attached to the office of a mayor, city manager, board of supervisors, or county executive. Typically, the line agency will have various operating responsibilities, whereas the staff agency will be essentially an advisory and a coordinating agency.

• Semi-public agencies: These may be public-benefit corporations or authorities. The common element is that they are created by a legislative act but are not part of the structure of government and have, at least in principle, some degree of autonomy. In addition to having the legal powers normally associated with private enterprises, such as the power to enter into contracts, such an organization may also have some powers normally associated with governments—for instance, the power to condemn land or the power to issue certain types of tax-exempt securities.

• Private/public partnerships: This category covers a very wide range. The organization may be a private entity, often organized as a not-for-profit corporation in which the public sector is represented through board membership. It may or may not have financial links to government, in that some part of its budget may come from the public treasury.

• Purely private groups: This category includes chambers of commerce, various city and county organizations. Funding is private and there are no formal links to government.

DESIRABLE CHARACTERISTICS FOR A DEVELOPMENT ORGANIZATION

One way to look at the type of structure to be preferred is to consider what the desirable characteristics are for an economic development organization. Some are listed below.

Pro-business orientation. This does not mean willingness to run roughshod over the public good. in pursuit of any business anywhere. But it does mean a generally cooperative and nonhostile attitude, some understanding of business and businessmen's concerns, and a capacity to establish rapport with businessmen.

Ability To Respond Rapidly. Both because time is money and because of the intense competitiveness of economic development, rapid response is important. The economic developer may feel frustrated when the businessman takes a year to think about a site and then appears in the office wanting to know, by the end of the week, whether the agency is willing to arrange financing for him. But that sort of situation is not infrequent. As a seller operating in a buyer's market, the economic developer has little choice but to accommodate himself to it.

Access to Government. The role of government in facilitating or obstructing development is a very big one. A wise pattern of public investment, particularly for roads and utilities, may greatly facilitate development. Unreasonable land-use controls, and long delays in the granting of permits can drive away investment and economic activity. In many cases, government financial participation is essential. This is particularly so in downtown redevelopment and in ventures of a quasi-public nature, such as convention centers. An agency which can cut through red tape, can guide firms through zoning, environmental, and other mazes, can get quick answers, and engage government in productive discussion is much to be desired.

Technical Capability. Economic development is hardly a science, nor is it likely to become one shortly. But there is room for technical competence in every major aspect of the process: developing market strategy, mounting a public-relations and advertising campaign, providing technical information, assisting firms in their dealings with local government and regulatory agencies, arranging financing, assisting in applications to state and federal agencies.

Credibility and Trustworthiness. In the long term, it is important for the development agency or agencies to have a reputation for not making promises that cannot be kept, for respecting confidences, and for generally being trustworthy and reliable.

Absence of Destructive Intraarea Competition. Very often the firm thinking about an area will find itself pulled in different directions by competing organizations within that jurisdiction, all seeking to be at the center of events and all seeking maximum credit for whatever does occur. That kind of competition can cause agencies to badmouth each other, to promise more than they can do, and to move in hasty and ill-conceived ways in order to steal a march upon the competition. A little competition may cause them all to make their best effort, but excessive competition is likely to be counterproductive from a community viewpoint.

The organizational structure of the economic development effort is likely to have less to do with how it measures up to the above points than with the character of the people involved, the funding available to it, and the general political climate in which it operates. But nonetheless, let us risk some general observations.

The public agency may have the advantage so far as political access goes. This is particularly likely if it is organized in such a way that it is directly linked to the top of the political structure. A development agency which is organized as part of the mayor's office, or as a separate line agency reporting directly to that office, may be very well positioned to engage the interest of the political structure when required and to get quick answers from government when they are needed.

But such close linkage can have its disadvantages. The operation can become so politicized that visibility becomes primary and actual accomplishment secondary. What appears in the press can become more important than what appears on the ground. Top positions in the agency may become filled with the politically deserving rather than the technically competent. Well-paid and highly visible economic development jobs can make nice plums to offer campaign contributors, party loyalists, those with useful political connections, or those to whom one is indebted for services rendered in the political wars of days gone by.

The public agency, whether staff or line, may have certain difficulties with regard to personnel selection. If hiring and promotion must be done through a civil-service structure, it may be very difficult to acquire people with enough private-sector background to understand and communicate adequately with businessmen. The problem is likely to be more acute where the economic development function is part of a line agency—for example, community development, planning, public works.

Where the economic development group is lodged in a larger department, it may benefit from the technical and staff support of the larger agency. For example, a development group attached to a planning agency may benefit from the agency's data analysis, planning and graphic capabilities, and perhaps, also, from the web of relationships the agency has built up with local officials over the years. Planning agencies are often very well equipped to provide technical support. On the other hand, the development group may find itself buried in an agency whose primary focus is otherwise, and it may thus find itself delayed and hampered when other agency goals take precedence. The same might be said for locating a development group in a major line agency like public works. The technical support may be useful at times, but the submergence of development concerns can be a definite problem. One economic development consultant with very wide experience notes, "It is a very bad idea to have those who do the regulating also do the promoting." Perhaps that is saying no more than, "No man can serve two masters."

In the most general sense, the public agency, staff or line, and particularly line, may be troubled by the traditional problems of bureaucracy and civil service—excessive caution, red tape, and inflexibility.

The semipublic agency may avoid some of the problems of the public agency; the excessive politicization is probably less likely to occur. As a nongovernmental agency, it may have somewhat less difficulty in achieving rapport with business. The greater freedom in hiring and firing that characterizes the private sector is likely to be an advantage. The semipublic agency or the private/public partnership agency may be capable of greater risk taking simply because its top people do not have to run for election. The creation of such an agency may give elected officials somewhat more latitude because they can disassociate themselves from situations in which the political heat becomes too intense. A county executive, for example, may feel that a certain development proposal makes sense for the county as a whole, but knows it may run into serious citizen opposition in the immediate environs. If the development agency is a public one, he may not take the risk. If the agency is politically separate, he may quietly encourage the proposal, knowing that if the citizens' opposition is too powerful, he can disassociate himself from the project without damage. In fact, he may then oppose the project and present himself as a knight in shining armor to the embattled citizenry. The writer has seen this maneuver done quite successfully. The semipublic or public partnership agency may also have some advantages in terms of achieving public support simply because its board includes representatives of major organizations and constituencies within the community. For these reasons, these types of agencies are to be found quite often.

There is much to be said for funding the semipublic agency from a combination of public and private sources. The contributing of money builds a commitment and creates an interest which may not otherwise be present. The agency may get much better cooperation from the business community if some portion of its funds come from local businesses than if all the funds come from the public purse. One development consultant of the author's acquaintance has taken the position, with some communities, that they should not set up a development organization unless some stipulated percentage of the total budget is forthcoming from business sources.

Because of the frequent need for the presence of government in the economic development process, the writer is inclined to see the purely private organization as likely to be somewhat less effective than the organization which has at least some links to the public sector. (There are, no doubt, exceptions to this, and many instances where formal links are absent but effective informal links exist.) Where the chamber of commerce fills the development role, there may be problems in that the economic development function may become submerged in other chamber concerns. Where a separate development group is to be found, there may be funding problems because both the development group and the chamber are attempting to raise funds from the same organizations. A group which is continually absorbed in the question of funding is obviously less able to devote effort to its fundamental goals. Then, too, the fear of alienating contributors may cause it to behave with excessive caution.

Agency staffing needs, regardless of whether the agency is public, semipublic, or private, will vary with the types of things the agency does.

Virtually any agency has some public-relations side to its operation and needs someone who can handle that aspect of the operation. An agency staffed entirely by technical people, with no one who could address a Rotary club, or write a press release, or make followup phone calls after an advertising campaign would be quite handicapped, particularly in its early years. In fact, very often, development agencies begin by being staffed largely with front men and then take on more technical people as inquiries come in and projects begin to materialize.

How much technical depth the agency requires depends on what it does. If the agency just serves a chamber-of-commerce function, but has no implementing or financing role, it may need only enough technical depth to build up a data base and answer some general questions on matters like taxation, utilities, zoning, the structure of local government. City or regional planning often provides an excellent background for doing that type of work. If the agency is involved in financing, it is essential to have some legal and financial expertise available. The expertise may be contained within the staff or may be on tap on a consulting or an advisory basis. The writer once operated a revenue-bond issuing agency whose ultimate financial and legal expertise resided, respectively, with two bankers on an unpaid board and with the agency's bond counsel. Full-time staff possessed enough understanding of financial and legal complexities to communicate with firms and to outline financial and legal arrangements in principle, but in no sense could be termed expert. The arrangement proved to be quite satisfactory.

If the agency actually performs a development function directly, meaning that it acquires property, markets parcels, negotiates leases, then capabilities in commercial real estate and property management are essential. At least some of these capabilities should be available on a more-or-less full-time basis. Physical planning may be contracted out to a planning or engineering consultant, because it can be done at one time, even though it may be periodically reviewed or monitored. If the agency is being formed as a branch of government that will have to hire under civil-service rules, it is important to see that position titles, job descriptions, and the entire personnel process are set up in such a way that the agency will be able to hire people with usable backgrounds. The types of skills mentioned above are not likely to be found within the established civil-service work force, and if the agency cannot break out of that structure for hiring purposes, it may be severely handicapped.

5

CHANGES IN THE PATTERN
OF ECONOMIC LOCATION

The pattern of economic location and the relative competitive position of various places have been changing rapidly in recent years. Areas once regarded as economic backwaters have taken off, and many once-thriving areas are now distressed areas. The migration of both people and jobs is rapidly changing the economic and social landscape of the nation. While an understanding of the forces behind these changes is not necessary for the day-to-day operation of a development agency, it is extremely helpful in thinking about larger questions of development strategy and marketing. Having a grasp of the main currents of economic change may help the economic developer distinguish between the inevitable, the possible, and the desirable but impossible—important distinctions to make when time, money, and legal and political powers are limited.

The major changes in the distribution and character of economic activity that have occurred since the end of World War II are generally well known. Population and employment in the Southeast and the Southwest have grown rapidly. In the Northeast and North Central sections of the country, the moderate growth of the 1950s and 1960s has been replaced by slow growth and, in some areas, shrinkage. The North-South disparity in wages and personal incomes has largely disappeared. In 1950, per capita income in Connecticut, the most prosperous New England state, was 161 percent greater than in Mississippi, the least prosperous southern state. By 1977, Mississippi was still the poorest southern state and Connecticut was still the most prosperous New England state, but the differential had shrunk to 61 percent. As Table 5.1 indicates, the income gap between North and South has closed substantially in the last three decades.

TABLE 5.1

Regional Per Capita Income as a Percent of National Per Capita Income

Region	1950	1977
New England	109.2	102.3
Mid-Atlantic	117.9	106.3
East North Central	111.4	104.6
West North Central	94.4	97.3
South Atlantic	80.6	93.1
East South Central	60.4	80.5
West South Central	79.9	92.0
Mountain	93.1	93.8
Pacific	120.3	111.4

Source: Bureau of the Census, *Statistical Abstract of the United States*, Dept. of Commerce, Washington, D.C., Government Printing Office, various years.

If adjustments are made for differences in cost of living and tax burden, the North-South income gap, for practical purposes, is gone.

Manufacturing, an activity which is of particular concern to the economic developer because of its export-base role (see Appendix A), was once heavily concentrated in what Thompson has called "the American Ruhr," a belt of industrialization stretching from New England to the upper Midwest.[1] As Table 5.2 indicates, there has been a major, and accelerating shift of manufacturing employment away from this area. Taking the New England, the Mid-Atlantic, and East North Central regions as an approximation of Thompson's "American Ruhr," the regions' combined share of total manufacturing employment dropped from 61.0 percent in 1958 to 57.3 percent in 1967 to 51.3 percent in 1976. In absolute terms, the regions lost almost 1.5 million manufacturing jobs from 1967 to 1976, while the remainder of the country gained about .9 million.

In the last several decades, metropolitan areas have absorbed the overwhelming share of both economic and population growth. But within metropolitan areas, there has been a steady relocation of people and jobs from central city to suburban ring. In many cases, jobs have moved out more rapidly than people, leaving in their wake poverty, unemployment, and despair. In both percentage and absolute terms, incomes in the suburban rings have grown more rapidly than in central cities, creating a steadily widening income gap between city and suburb. The economic decline and fiscal crisis of older urban areas is now an old story to the most casual newspaper reader.

TABLE 5.2

Regional Shifts in Manufacturing Employment (figures in 000s)

Region	Manufacturing Employment			Absolute Change, 1967–76	1976 as Percent of 1967
	1958	1967	1976		
New England	1,399	1,562	1,336	−266	85.5
Mid-Atlantic	4,110	4,360	3,501	−859	80.3
East North Central	4,260	5,151	4,786	−365	92.9
West North Central	963	1,206	1,268	62	105.1
South Atlantic	1,889	2,502	2,732	230	109.0
East South Central	783	1,092	1,296	204	118.7
West South Central	797	1,083	1,353	270	124.9
Mountain	229	315	439	124	139.3
Pacific	1,594	2,050	2,064	14	100.6
United States	16,025	19,323	18,753	−570	97.0

Source: Bureau of the Census, *Statistical Abstract of the United States,* Washington, D.C., Government Printing Office, various years.

Manufacturing activity, the economic backbone of many cities, has been moving out at a rapid pace. Some of this movement has merely been a shift from city to suburban ring. But much of it has been movement to other regions of the country. And much of the migration of light industry has been to small towns and rural areas far from major metropolitan centers. Retailing, another traditional mainstay of the central-city economy, has also moved out at a rapid pace, further adding to the employment and revenue problems of the cities.

In the production and distribution of many types of goods, regional markets have been supplanted by national and, in many cases, international markets. Nationally, the economy is far more open to the rest of the world than it was two decades ago. Exports and imports rose from about 3.9 and 2.9 percent of GNP, respectively, in 1960 to about 6.4 and 8.0 percent of GNP, respectively, in 1977.[2] While the United States remains predominant in the manufacture of many high-technology products and many capital goods, it is finding it increasingly difficult to compete in many types of consumer products, a fact which is quite significant to the economic distress felt by many older urban areas.

Internally, a vast migration has occurred. America's black population, once predominantly rural and heavily concentrated in the Southeast, is now more highly urbanized than the nation's white population. The cities of the Northeast and North Central areas are now the repository of an often impoverished black population, much as the rural South was in the days of the Great Depression. The migration appears to have ended in the mid 1970s. Some apparent causes for the cessation are the relative economic decline of the North relative to the South, the improvement in the civil-rights situation in the South, and the slowing in the rate of decline in agricultural employment. But its effects will be felt for many decades.[3] A reverse movement, the migration of whites from the Northeast and North Central states to the Sunbelt states, has been going on for some years. But, unlike the black migration to the North, it shows no signs of stopping.

While no single explanation can account for all that has been observed, one can point to a single factor which may serve as an organizing principle. This factor is technological change. In a most direct sense, technological change alters the relative costs of doing business and living in various areas and thus promotes inter- and intraarea movement of people and jobs. At one remove, technological change may explain some demographic changes, the changing relationship of the United States and world economies, and perhaps even some rather significant changes in taste and habit.

At the risk of treading on familiar ground, let us look briefly at the relationship between technology and the location of commerce and industry. At the turn of the century, transportation by water and rail was cheap and other modes were relatively quite expensive. The combination of 19th-century transportation technology and the labor requirements of factories and that newly developed mercantile institution, the corporate headquarters, necessarily concentrated people and jobs in densely developed urban areas. Two innovations in building technology appearing shortly after the Civil War—steel-frame construction and the elevator— facilitated the trend to high urban densities.

The development of automotive technology in the 20th century drastically changed the economics of transportation for both goods and people. The importance of docks and railheads as centers of economic activity was greatly reduced, and workers were able to live at much greater distances from their jobs. A process of spreading out was begun, and has continued to the present time.

The diffusing effect of automotive technology was aided and abetted by other changes in technology, some related and some not related. The development of the assembly line and other straight-through manufacturing processes favored one-story over multistory plants, thus obsoleting loft buildings and placing a premium on areas where land costs were low enough to permit spread-out one-story construction. The limited-access highway (an invention of the 1920s) decreased automotive travel times in the suburban ring and facilitated the movement of population and employment into the ring. The building of the interstate highway system (conceived in the 1930s and started in the 1950s) greatly increased the accessibility of small cities and nonmetropolitan areas. By increasing point-to-point trucking speeds, the system has also generally weakened the competitive position of railroads, with powerful decentralizing consequences. Improvements in shipping technology, such as containerization, coupled with improved transportation technology, have reduced the cost of transportation relative to that of production. The result has been to decrease the importance of centrality and to favor continued decentralization. Modern electronics has also favored decentralization. Anything which permits people to communicate at a distance reduces the need for them to be physically close. Communications technology advanced slowly during the first few decades of the 20th century and then, propelled by wartime advances followed by the invention of the transistor in 1948, has moved with incredible speed. Semiconductor technology (transistor, integrated circuit, microprocessor) may well be as much a diffuser of economic activity and of population as the automobile and motor truck. Long-distance direct dialing, facsimile transmission, computer-to-computer data links over common carriers, closed-circuit TV, and other devices all make possible further decentralization of economic activity. The process is far from over. As of this writing, there is considerable interest, in banking and financial circles, in electronic funds transfer (EFT). This may well have the effect of weakening the relative strength of existing financial centers since, for example, checks will clear with the same speed regardless of location. A combination of laser technology and fiber optics now in process of moving from the prototype to production stage promises huge increases in data-transmission capability, with consequences which cannot be foreseen. It is widely expected that in the 1980s the continued lowering in the cost of computing power and communications will make it possible for many professionals to work at home. The probable effect will be further decentralization.

The synergistic quality of improvements in transportation and communications technology seems evident. The movement of manufacturing out of cities and into nonmetropolitan areas is a case in point. The motor truck and the interstate highway provided access to markets and raw materials. The automobile provided access to a dispersed rural and small-town labor force. Electronics provided instantaneous communications to distant headquarters for branches and subsidiaries. Advances in the speed, safety, and all-weather capability of general aviation aircraft made it possible for corporate officers to travel easily from headquarters in metropolitan areas to formerly remote rural and small-town branches. (Although there are over 10,000 airports in the United States, fewer than 600 have scheduled service. A trip from, say, New York City to western North Carolina by scheduled airline, which would be an overnight event complete with changes of plane and a long auto trip, might be completed by corporate jet or turboprop in an hour or two.) Granted that motivation to relocate had to be present (low wages, ununionized labor forces, lower land and construction costs), the trend could not have occurred without a combination of facilitating technologies.

Agricultural technology has produced remarkable changes in the labor force of the United States. In this century, output per worker in agriculture has actually increased more rapidly than in industry. In 1940, approximately 10 million agricultural workers fed a U.S. population of 130 million and produced some surplus for export. By the late 1970s, under 4 million workers fed 220 million people and produced an enormous surplus for export.

The mechanization of agriculture that accelerated rapidly during the Great Depression produced an internal migration comparable in size to the external immigration the United States experienced in the period preceding World War I. Metropolitan areas, particularly those of the Northeast and North Central regions, received a vast migration of now-surplus agricultural workers. At the same time, falling rural populations caused the economic stagnation of many thriving small towns. For many small towns, the effect was compounded by increasingly widespread automobile ownership. The spacing of towns is largely a function of travel time. Thus, as higher-speed modes of transportation become available, any given area could be served by a smaller number of central places. Thus, a few nodal places grew, or at least maintained themselves, while many less favorably situated places atrophied. A third factor contributing to the economic malaise of some rural areas has been changing demand for raw materials. In Appalachia, the shift from coal to oil that occurred after World War II impoverished many places for which coal was the main export industry. (Given the increases in oil prices since the early 1970s, this trend appears on the verge of reversal.)

In an earlier age, the influx of unskilled labor might have strengthened the economic position of the cities receiving it. But the influx arrived in a period when the need for unskilled labor was shrinking. Increasing productivity and the growing sophisticated of the production process reduced the need for willing but unskilled and poorly educated workers. The Eastern European immigrant to New York or Boston in 1910 found a much more easily penetrable labor market than did the black immigrant arriving in, say, 1960.

Thus, rather than strengthening the economic position of the cities, as had been true of earlier waves of immigration, the new influx weakened them. A rapid increase in the needs for a wide range of social services drove up tax rates and starved other municipal services. Increases in crime, and in class and race conflict, and deterioration in other public services, most notably education, accelerated the flight of the white working and middle classes. Firms were encouraged to follow their workers and their customers to the suburbs. Thus, to the pull of improving transportation and communications technology, was added the push of increased taxation and a deteriorating quality of life. As noted earlier, the black migration to the central cities is over, but the white flight shows no signs of abating.[4]

Ironically, after having accepted an exodus of poor blacks from the South, many northern cities find themselves losing manufacturing activity to the South. But, as has been noted by other writers, the movement of manufacturing from the North to the South is to predominantly white areas such as the Piedmont of Virginia and the Carolinas. According to Thompson, "There are a number of reasons for this new form of racial discrimination. . . . Relocating manufacturers find the hill country white workers are free thinkers who reject unions, while black workers seek the protection of unions. With white labor, there is neither a union problem nor a racial problem."[5] The influence of technology is clear, for it is the truck, the auto, and the limited-access highway that permit manufacturers to settle in the once-isolated nonmetropolitan community.

Beyond technology, though often related to it, are a number of factors that have influenced economic location, and of which it is well for the economic developer to be aware.

Interarea wage differentials in the United States have had a significant effect on the location and relocation of firms. The well-known wage gap between the North and South has now largely closed, but in the past has been a major force in pulling industry southward. Today, the big wage differential is not between the North and South but between metropolitan and nonmetropolitan locations. The substantially lower wage levels of nonmetropolitan areas, coupled with the improvements in transportation and communications mentioned before, are a major force in the nonmetropolitan movement in manufacturing.

In time, metropolitan-versus-nonmetropolitan wage differentials may narrow as the labor surpluses of nonmetropolitan areas are gradually absorbed. But this has yet to happen. As Thompson notes, the labor pools of many rural areas have proved "surprisingly deep," in part because former residents who had migrated to major cities are often eager to come back when job opportunities permit.[6] Thus, increases in employment may not bid up wages to nearly the extent they would were the labor supply relatively inelastic.

Cost-of-living differentials, generally favoring southern and nonmetropolitan locations, have obviously encouraged the movement of population and jobs in those directions. Not only are workers and retirees (who bring their transfer-payment incomes with them) more readily attracted to low-cost areas, but employers find such areas attractive because lower living costs translate into lower wages. The progressivity of the federal income tax heightens the advantage of the low-living-cost area. In net terms, one is better off with a $20,000 income in an area with a cost-of-living index of 80 than with a $25,000 income in an area with a cost-of-living index of 100, a condition which would not be the case were federal taxes not progressive.

Tax burdens vary widely by state and, to a lesser degree, by substate area. Academic studies of the effect of tax differentials (largely done in the 1960s and early 1970s conclude that tax differentials figure only lightly in determining industrial and commercial location. On the basis of conversations with representatives of firms, this writer has never been fully convinced of the truth of this conclusion. Then, too, as local taxes have risen as a percentage of GNP, comparable percentage differences in tax burden become larger absolute differences. Thus, it may well be that old studies, if redone, would show larger effects.

Regardless of the precise importance of differential tax rates, one can see a circular relationship. High tax rates reduce the level of economic activity. The costs of government do not fall by a comparable amount, and thus still higher rates are necessary. Further losses of economic activity occur and the cycle is repeated.[7]

New York State, which has fared very badly in the competition for industry in the last decade, has had, until recently, the highest tax burden in the nation.[8] Precisely the above relationship between taxes and industrial growth has been postulated, and the state has recently made serious efforts to reduce taxes.

The structure of taxes, as well as the absolute amount, may also affect economic location. For example, a highly progressive tax structure places the greatest burden on the affluent. This appears socially desirable to the liberal perspective, and also has the advantage that its net burden within the state is smaller because of deductibility against a progressive federal income tax. Thus, in terms of the export-base model presented in Appendix A, it appears superior to a proportional or regressive system. But it has the disadvantage that it falls most heavily on those who make locational decisions. New York, in spite of a strong liberal political tradition, recently cut back the top rate on the state income tax from 15 to 12 percent for exactly this reason.

In general, no tax is entirely neutral in its effect among various industries. For any given level of revenues raised, different tax structures will favor different industry mixes. A gross-receipts tax, for example, falls more heavily upon wholesalers than manufacturers. A sales tax on electricity falls more heavily on electroplaters (an energy-intensive activity) than on sheet-metal fabricators.

Southern states have typically had both smaller total tax burdens and less progressive (or more regressive) tax structures. How much this had aided them in the competition for industry is not certain, but it seems unarguable that it has been of some assistance. It is widely believed that the North's usually more generous levels of public expenditure for social services and education, coupled with the higher tax burdens this required, have helped to promote the flow of industry from the North to the South and the flow of poor people from the South to the North. The population side of this flow exchange appears to have ended sometime in the mid 1970s with the closing of North-South wage differentials and the prevalence of generally lower unemployment rates in many parts of the South. Its effects, however, will continue to be felt for many years. The southward flow of jobs continues unabated.[9]

The overall pattern of federal expenditure has often been cited as a major force in determining economic location. While the federal government spends some money, primarily through HUD and EDA, with the express intention of altering the location of economic activity, much larger sums spent for other purposes have locational effects. Studies which contrast federal taxes collected, by state, with federal expenditures, by state, show a pattern in which many northeastern and north central states are "capital exporters" while a number of southeastern and southwestern states are "capital importers."[10]

In fiscal 1975, the Northeast and the Midwest were net exporters to the extent of approximately $31 billion while the South and West were net importers by about $22 billion. (The difference occurs because the District of Columbia is treated separately. Were it added to the totals from the South, the account would balance.) Among the big losers in this process were New York ($3.4 billion), Ohio ($4.6 billion), Illinois ($5.3 billion), Michigan ($5.0 billion) and New Jersey ($4.4 billion). Among the big winners were California ($3.7 billion), Virginia ($2.6 billion), Maryland ($1.3 billion), New Mexico ($1.0 billion), and Washington ($2.0 billion). The biggest source of variation was defense expenditure. The spending of federal money for defense installations, military procurement, research and development, in a direct sense, constitutes export activity. Indirectly, it ofteñ builds such great levels of expertise that the area becomes predominant in comparable nongovernmental production as well. Electronics and aviation are cases in point.

Since the 1973 Arab oil embargo, increasing energy costs have had a number of effects on the location of economic activity. While the total picture is not yet clear, some major effects have occurred. Some of these are direct results of price changes. Others stem from governmental responses to price changes. In some cases, it is hard to untangle the two.

Rising energy prices have obviously favored a limited number of resource-rich states. Beyond that, they have generally favored the South over the North. First, but not necessarily foremost, as the cost of heating rises, colder areas necessarily exhibit higher absolute increases in heating costs. This is likely to have a direct effect on industrial location simply because it changes operating-cost structures. Then, too, for both commercial and residential use, money expended on fuel produced outside the area in question represents a leakage from the flow of money in the local or regional economy.

Coincidentally, it happens that the North has generally relied upon oil for a larger percentage of its total energy supply than has the South. Conversely, the South has relied more heavily upon natural gas than has the North. As of the end of January 1980, natural gas sold to industrial users at about $2.37 per 1,000 cubic feet (roughly 1 million BTUs). At the same time, oil used for industrial heating sold for $26.26 per barrel, or about $4.53 per 1 million BTUs.[11] In short, a manufacturer in the Sunbelt, running on natural gas, was paying only 53 percent as much, per unit of energy, as his northern competitor was paying by running on oil. The relative differential between oil and gas prices on a BTU basis has existed for some years. But as the price of all forms of energy rises, the absolute value of any percentage difference necessarily rises.

From a northern viewpoint, the problem has been compounded by federal regulations. These controlled the price of natural gas in interstate commerce but did not control it in intrastate commerce. Thus, a pattern of interstate shortages and intrastate surpluses developed. This, coupled with the fact that much gas supply is tied up in long-term contracts, has made it difficult for northern firms or homeowners to switch to gas.

Another facet of the energy question is the income to be realized from royalties and severance charges. As energy prices rise, states which contain substantial energy resources are able to levy very large charges on the use of state lands and on resources extracted. (The term "severance" comes from the levying of a tax when the raw material is "severed" from the earth.) Constitutional prohibitions on restraint of interstate commerce would forbid taxing materials destined for out-of-state sale differently than materials destined for intrastate sale. However, a tax uniformly applied to a resource, the preponderance of which is sold out of state, in effect permits the material-possessing state to tax the citizens of other states. In terms of either the capital-export concept mentioned earlier or the export-base model discussed in Appendix A, the increased severance tax and royalty incomes that higher energy prices permit will greatly favor a limited number of states rich in oil and coal. Recent estimates place prospective revenues from these sources at several hundred billion dollars for the 1980s. The potential effects on the location of economic activity are enormous.

As a harbinger of things to come, the state of Alaska has eliminated its state income tax entirely and is now making refunds on previous years' taxes to residents on the basis of revenues from north-slope oil.

As noted before, international trade as a percentage of U.S. GNP has almost doubled in the last two decades. The diffusion of manufacturing technology, and the general lowering of tariffs and other artificial barriers to international trade have opened up many U.S. markets to strong international competition. While the United States still holds a superior position in many high-technology products (main-frame computers, aircraft, automated machine tools), it has lost ground over a very wide range of consumer goods (apparel, shoes, bicycles, automobiles, consumer electronics). Areas such as California's "Silicon Valley" have not been hurt by the growth of international trade and international markets. In fact, they may have been helped by the expanding demand for their high-technology output. But places like New York's garment district have been seriously damaged by it. The economic developer whose vision does not extend beyond national boundaries is likely to miss both opportunities and threats.

Since the late 1970s, the arcane world of exchange rates and international currency flows has assumed an importance for the local economic developer. In theory, if a dollar exchanges for two deutsche marks, it is because one dollar in the United States will buy about as much as will two deutsche marks in Germany. In fact, however, by the criteria of equivalent buying power, the U.S. dollar is generally conceded to be significantly undervalued. Why this condition exists may be the subject of some argument. It has been suggested that it is the inevitable result of the huge "overhang" of Eurodollars built up over many years. Critics of American monetary and fiscal policies have argued that it is the result of imprudent public spending and excessive money creation. But regardless of the cause, the fact of the dollar's undervaluation seems clear. Undervaluation, coupled with the social and political stability of the United States, has made U.S. real estate a bargain to many individuals and firms outside the United States. Beyond that, many European and Japanese firms are finding that it is cheaper to produce in the United States, for the U.S. market, than to export the finished product to the United States. The result has been an increasing amount of reverse investment. The labor-cost advantage which Japan and many European producers enjoyed vis-à-vis the United States has been largely dissipated by the combination of rising real income at home and the undervaluation of the dollar internationally. Very often, foreign firms find that the combination of producing parts at home but assembling them here is the lowest-cost combination when wages, shipping costs, and tariffs are considered in total. In some areas, reverse investment may have rather dramatic effects. In Manhattan, rentals of what is referred to by brokers as "class A" office space have roughly tripled in the last half-decade. It is believed that a substantial part of the increase in demand is from one or another type of reverse investment.

For the economic developer, the fact of reverse investment opens up many possibilities for industrial and commercial recruitment. In terms of marketing operations, headquarters of U.S. subsidiaries, and the like, major cities on the East and West Coasts clearly have an advantage. In terms of manufacturing operations, many other locations within the United States are able to compete for reverse investment. The number of states sending trade delegations to Western Europe and Japan is clear evidence that this opportunity is not being overlooked.

Climate and quality of life have in recent years become far more important factors than was previously the case in the determining of economic locations. The link between this observation and changing technology may not be immediately apparent, but it can easily be suggested.

Consider several factors, all of which are either directly attributable to technological change or which can be traced back to it through a very short chain of reasoning:

● major increases in real per capita GNP (from 1929 to 1973, real per capita GNP in the United States almost tripled);
● decreasing costs of transportation relative to the costs of production;
● the emergence of a variety of tertiary and high-technology industries in which ability to recruit specialized personnel is a key element in production and in competition between firms;
● the decreasing percentage of the labor force employed in heavy industry, agriculture, and raw-materials extraction and processing;
● the development of air conditioning.

All of these have made amenities, whether they be amenities of climate, lifestyle, or some specialized taste, far more important than before in the location of economic activity. An affluent population need not be bound by the forces of economic necessity to the extent that a poor one is. The growth of places as different as Boulder, St. Petersburg, or southern California springs in large measure from the freedom of an affluent population to live where it wants to, rather than where it has to. The migration of firms may thus often follow the migration of people, rather than leading it. The increasing percentage of the population employed in activities which do not involve a great deal of bulk transport permits locational decisions to be made relatively independent of transportation costs. An activity like steel manufacture, in which several tons of raw materials must be brought together to produce one ton of finished product worth only a few hundred dollars, must locate, to a great degree, on the basis of transportation costs. But the development of computer software can be sited quite independent of the cost of materials transport.

The movement of corporate-headquarters activity out of central cities into the suburbs is another exercise of preference modern technology permits. The writer, at one time, had some involvement with a very large commodity-brokerage firm that moved from the financial district in lower Manhattan to an office park in the suburbs. The firm's officers had wanted to make the move for some time, for reasons largely related to the residential preferences of top personnel. As soon as the necessary data and voice-communications links became available outside the city, they moved. The firm is a perfect example of the freedom in choice of location technology has conferred. It is a tertiary operation in which no physical product is made or handled. All it needs for its operation is personnel and communications.

Many who work in economic development are surprised in due time by the extent to which the residential preferences of top corporate officials influence the choice of location. This is particularly true of headquarters operations. This, too, is a kind of freedom technology permits. Were it not possible to operate with roughly similar efficiency from a variety of locations, that freedom would not exist.

When a firm considers whether to remain in a central business district or to move several dozen miles into suburbia, it is considering an option which has been made possible by an array of technologies—the automobile, the limited-access highway, low-cost electronic communications, closed-circuit TV, facsimile transmission, high-performance general aviation aircraft.

In terms of selling an area, the economic developer quickly finds that quality of life can be the determining issue with many types of firms. The quality of public education, the feeling of personal safety, the presence of parks and country clubs, a pleasant climate, a scenically attractive environment, the proximity of marinas or ski slopes, and a prestige location all weigh in the locational decisions of many types of firms. That they do weigh heavily is because technology has removed many constraints of time and distance.

Since this chapter has been written around technological change as the central principle, a few words about the future might be appropriate here. No prophecy is offered; rather, a few comments about possibilities.

Obviously, electronic communications facilities are still improving rapidly, and no end to the communications revolution is in sight. It will continue to be a decentralizing force. If a great deal of tertiary activity can be transferred to the home, making various kinds of intellectual and information-based work the cottage industry of the future, its effects on the location of economic activity may be very powerful.

Increasing energy prices (measured in real terms) may have a contrary effect. It is widely believed that the energy crisis will have a strong reurbanizing effect on the United States. Whether we will, in fact, reurbanize or whether we will make other adaptations to increased energy costs strikes this writer as unknowable at this time. Energy shortages have been neither severe enough nor prolonged enough to produce sufficient effects upon which to base judgment. It is possible that increasing energy costs will favor urban areas generally, and in particular, those urban areas with highly developed public transportation systems. Certainly the economic developer in Boston, New York, or Chicago could use the possession of well-developed public-transportation systems as a powerful selling point.

Whether the United States chooses the hard or the soft path, in terms of power generation, may have huge consequences for the location of economic activity and the relative competitiveness of different regions of the country. A major turn toward solar energy, for example, could have profoundly antiurban consequences, for cloud cover, northern latitudes, and shadows are major enemies of solar energy. Thus, solar power will probably favor the Southeast and Southwest over the more urbanized North. Other soft technologies, such as wind and geothermal power, may also work better in less densely developed areas where interference effects are minimized.

Cogeneration (the use of otherwise waste heat from power generation for space heating and industrial processes) is an emerging technology. It may well promote patterns of industrial, commercial, and residential development whose nature will become clear only with the passage of time. Suffice it to say, then, that for the economic developer, there may be little on this score that can be said definitely, but much that bears watching.

NOTES

1. See the chapter by Wilbur Thompson in *Post-Industrial America: Metropolitan Decline and Inter-Regional Jobs Shifts*, George Sternlieb and James W. Hughes, eds., State University of New Jersey, Rutgers, New Brunswick, 1975.

2. Calculation is from Bureau of the Census, *Statistical Abstract of the United States*, Washington, D.C., Government Printing Office, 1960, 1977.

3. While black net migration (moves in minus moves out) has ended, the black populations will grow relative to white populations for several decades. This is largely because black urban populations tend to be much younger than white urban populations and therefore exhibit a much higher rate of natural increase.

4. The racial transition in many central cities has also hastened the move out by a number of firms, particularly headquarters and other operations with large clerical requirements, for reasons which no large firm will admit publicly. The firm's motivations prior to moving, or its experiences after having moved, may be discussed in somewhat vague terms, such as "labor-force quality" or "quality of life for our employees." Perversely, federal equal opportunity requirements may accelerate the trend because the requirements use, as a base figure, the minority percentage of the labor force in the particular labor-market area. Thus, the firm which moves from, say, Manhattan or downtown Chicago to a suburban location 30 miles away now has much smaller minority-recruitment goals to meet.

5. Thompson, op. cit.

6. Ibid.

7. Increasing population brings with it increases in total service costs and often some increase in per capita costs. But, increases in per capita costs are often balanced by increases in per capita income. In declining areas, total costs tend to decrease less slowly than population because of large fixed, or at least relatively inflexible, elements in the public cost

structure. Thus, shrinkage often presents far more intractable fiscal problems than growth. See the chapter by Thomas Muller in Sternlieb and Hughes, op. cit.

8. Two common measurements of fiscal burden are taxes per capita and taxes as a percentage of total personal income. The state leads all other states by both of these measures. See *New York State Yearbook*.

9. The term "flow" in this use is not meant in a literal sense. If a firm in New Jersey opens a plant in South Carolina and then, five years later, shuts down its operation in New Jersey, there has literally been no movement of jobs. The effect is quite similar, though, to a literal movement. The so-called flow of manufacturing from the North to the South has much more been a matter of differential rates of firm growth and shutdown that it has of literal movement.

10. "Where the Funds Flow." *National Tax Journal*, June 26, 1976.

11. *Monthly Energy Review*, May 1980, Dept. of Energy.

6

ASSESSING ECONOMIC
DEVELOPMENT POTENTIAL

The most appropriate place to begin planning an economic development program is with a realistic assessment of the development potential of the area. Such an assessment provides guidance for the expenditure of the development agency's necessarily limited money, energy, and legal and political powers. No initial assessment will prove entirely accurate. As the economic developer has contact with firms, brokers, bankers, property owners, and others, his insight into the area will increase. Unanticipated strengths and opportunities, weaknesses and problems, will emerge. Thus, like most plans, the initial assessment is meant to be modified. Nonetheless, a general assessment of the area's strengths and weaknesses should be undertaken either before the agency is founded or, if not, early in the history of the agency. Once the agency is in full operation, time for research and planning will be hard to come by.

A systematic evaluation of the area's strengths and weaknesses will not only help in planning, but will also provide a basis for justifying, defending, and explaining the program, both to the public and within the councils of government.

An unrealistic view of an area's potential leads to wasted effort, expectations which cannot be met, and ultimate disillusionment. Admittedly, the political climate is often such that the economic developer cannot be absolutely candid with his employers or the citizenry in general. A certain note of obligatory optimism seems to come with the territory. But he can at least look at the facts as objectively as possible for his own purposes.

In assessing strengths and weaknesses, it is important to consider matters from the point of view not only of the area's ability to attract new firms, but also its ability to retain and encourage the expansion of existing industry.

Very often agencies begin by focusing on the more glamorous business of bringing in new industry, only to discover in time that their most useful work is done with existing industry. A rule of thumb among economic developers is that 80 percent of economic growth is locally generated. While this may not literally be true, the message it conveys is a useful one.

The process of assessment suggested here is a three-part one: a general evaluation of major characteristics of the area; a consideration, in broad terms, of the types of economic activities most and least able to prosper in the area in terms of the findings of step one; a look at recent area trends to see whether the results of the initial assessment conform to the realities of recent economic trends.

GENERAL EVALUATION

In this first stage, it is suggested the economic developer make a brief reconnaissance, partly from published sources and partly from personal interviews, of a limited number of essential topics. The following generally weigh heavily in the initial locational choices by firms: location and transportation; labor markets; quality of life; political climate; energy costs; taxation; land availability and development costs; demographic characteristics. A brief discussion of each of these categories follows.

Location and Transportation

This is a question which has a number of dimensions. On a large scale, one should consider access to major metropolitan areas. One commonly used statistic is population within "overnight trucking distance."[1] The term does not have a precise meaning, but for an area with reasonable access to an interstate highway, one might calculate the population within a 500-mile radius. For other-than heavy industry, at the time of this writing, highway accessibility is more important than access by any other means. Given that rail transportation is three to four times as energy efficient on a ton-mile basis, this statement will not necessarily be true some years hence.[2]

Thus, some evaluation of rail access should also be made. Links and distances to major concentrations of population can readily be determined from maps. Beyond that, some determination should be made as to whether there are any special limitations. For example, trailer on flat car is a particularly economical way to ship for many firms because it retains much of the flexibility of trucking while achieving the lower per-mile costs of rail. But it requires larger clearances on tunnels and overpasses, and special loading and unloading facilities. A few conversations with shippers will turn up particular and nonobvious, but often significant details.

As a determinant of economic location, water transportation is generally less significant than either truck or rail, except in a limited number of industries where bulk transportation costs are very significant. (Barge and freighter are the most energy-efficicient modes on a ton-mile basis.) Nonetheless, for a place with a coastal or river location, the question should not be ignored. Beyond what can be seen from looking at maps, some inquiry should be made as to limitations posed by channel depths and loading facilities. For example, not every port which can accommodate oceangoing vessels has the facilities to accept container-ized freight, San Francisco being a case in point.

Access by air should also be considered. Here, one should break the inquiry into two parts. One is the condition of scheduled service to major destinations. The other is the presence and adequacy of general-aviation facili-ties. For a number of types of activity, adequate access by air is essential. The point is discussed in more detail later in this chapter.

After considering access with regard to other areas, access within the area in question should be considered. Does the area in question have an advantage or disadvantage vis-à-vis competing places in the same area? For example, in the New York area, two suburban counties, Nassau and Suffolk, with a combined population of about 2.5 million, are located on Long Island. Their only road access to the rest of the United States is through New York City via bridges and tunnels. In spite of good labor forces, somewhat lower-than-average wage rates for the region, available land, and many quality-of-life advantages, the two coun-ties have been generally unable to compete with other suburban counties in the region for many types of office and manufacturing employment. The access problem is apparently the main, if not only, reason. This type of intraarea access advantage or disadvantage will generally be apparent from maps or just from the experience of living in the area. But, again, a few conversations with major em-ployers and shippers may ferret out aspects of the situation that are not immedi-ately apparent.

Labor Markets

Most studies of industrial location indicate that the two biggest considera-tions in making a general choice of area are access to markets and access to labor.[3] (Within a given area, other factors wil then determine the final choice of municipality and site.) At least four dimensions of the labor market should be considered: wage rates, quality, availability, and unionization and legislation.

The most useful wage comparisons are those which show typical wages for different areas by occupation. Nationally, the best source for such information is provided by the *Area Wage Surveys.*[4] These provide average wages, median wages, and hours worked for about 40 different occupations, for major metropolitan areas. They are useful in determining a particular area's wage-rate competitiveness, when starting a development program, and may also be useful later on in preparing promotional materials and/or a data base (see Chapter 8). Within any given state, some of the same types of material may be provided by state labor departments. Monthly wage comparisons on a state and a major-labor-market basis are available in *Employment and Earnings.*[5] Unfortunately, they are limited to an average figure for production workers in manufacturing establishments.

Like most other sources of data on wages, the *Area Wage Surveys* focus on jobs which are relatively standardized and therefore comparable. Forklift operators in Chicago do very much the same work as forklift operators in Fargo, North Dakota. The same is not necessarily true for attorneys or managers. Thus, when one considers managerial, professional, and some technical workers, firm statistical comparability is not possible, and one is thrown back on the impressions of employers, personnel directors, employment-agency personnel. But impressions often deterrmine decisions, so a little time spent gathering such impressions should prove worthwhile.

For an overview of trends in labor markets nationally, there are a number of publications available. Two that may be useful are *Manpower Review* and *Occupational Outlook*, both published by the Bureau of Labor Statistics, Department of Labor.

Labor-force quality is the most subjective of the four labor dimensions listed earlier. In some development advertising, one will see value added per worker put forth as an indicator of labor-force quality. In reality, this is a measure of capital intensity more than anything else. Number of years of education of the adult population (a census-data item) is sometimes used as a measure of overall labor-force quality. Its meaning is questionable. Not only is the statistic not available by occupation, but beyond that, the link between years of schooling and job performance is not necessarily a rigid one. Here, perhaps more than in any other area, we are thrown back on impressions. Employers' perceptions of labor quality are a major factor in decision making and thus are worth gathering.

Even within relatively small areas, employers may perceive large differences in labor-force quality. The writer, working in a county of 450 square miles, was surprised to find that manufacturers saw large qualitative differences in the labor markets of communities only a few miles apart. These were differences which were in no way apparent from any available statistics, and yet the views of different employers were sufficiently consistent to convince the writer that they represented something real.

Labor Availability

Some data on the labor force and its composition in terms of major categories of workers are available from the decennial census.[6] The census is taken in years ending with 0 and published statistics become available in the following year. Fortunately, for most areas, the occupational mix of the population will not change abruptly over the period, so that this type of data does not age too rapidly. Then, too, as one gets further away in time from the last census, some projections can be made.

Unemployment rates are another dimension of labor availability.[7] The overall rate conveys some meaning, and rates by occupation, if available, convey more. But one should not make too much of the number of workers apparently available on the basis of unemployment figures. For many firms, the size of the labor pool is a better indication of long-term availability than is the apparent number of available workers on a given day. For one thing, hiring is a competitive process. For a second, the size of the labor force is somewhat inflexible. Within the geographical area, workers move into and out of the labor pool and move from one category of work to another within the pool. Then, too, job availability promotes migration.

When the writer was engaged in economic development in a suburb whose population was growing slowly, but which was experiencing very rapid growth of corporate-headquarters activity, all available data showed very tight markets for secretarial and clerical workers. In a period in which the female working-age population grew by perhaps 40 percent, clerical and secretarial employment in the area nearly doubled. From looking at numbers, it seemed inevitable that shortages of such workers were on the verge of choking off further corporate growth. Yet new corporate headquarters continued to move in and generally reported satisfaction with the labor market. The labor supply was obviously much more elastic than the statistics suggested. What was happening? New firms, by offering additional jobs, pushed up female labor-force participation rates. In addition, county residents who had previously worked outside the county began working closer to home. Finally, in-commutation from adjacent counties that had experienced relatively faster population growth, but relatively slower corporate-headquarters growth, increased. A damaging shortfall in secretarial and clerical labor was always imminent, but never materialized. Labor-force calculations are of considerable interest and use, but it must be remembered that the size of the labor force is not an absolutely rigid quantity. (The other side of this point, as noted earlier, is that employment gains may lower unemployment rates less than expected.)

Another source of insight into labor-market conditions is provided by job banks maintained by state employment agencies. Such banks may contain information on job vacancies posted by employers and on the occupations of job seekers. Also available from state labor departments are data on the characteristics of unemployment-insurance recipients.[8] These data can be used to quickly locate occupations in which there are obvious labor surpluses.

Finally, at the risk of repetition, the economic developer trying to assemble a picture of his area's labor market would do well to talk with employers and employment agencies. Those who are involved daily in the labor market often have insights which are not obtainable from statistics alone. Given the generally favorable growth attitudes of businessmen, the economic developer should have little difficulty persuading local employers to communicate with him.

Both unionization and protective labor legislation perform many useful functions. Making an area attractive to potential employers is not, however, one of these functions. In general, whether or not a city or state is a strong union area will be well known, both to management and labor. The economic developer will have little difficulty ascertaining his own area's reputation. New York, Pennsylvania, New England, for example, are generally regarded as strong union areas. Most southern states are not. If hard data on the degree of unionization are required, they can be obtained from the *Statistical Abstract of the United States*.

The situation regarding labor legislation, from the economic developer's point of view, can readily be determined by communication with employers, unions, and state labor departments. One piece of legislation which has become quite well known is the so-called right-to-work law. Essentially, this forbids making union membership a condition of employment; that is, it prohibits the union shop. It is typically found in states of a generally conservative political complexion, for example, Kansas. It would be anathema in a state of strongly liberal persuasion, such as Massachusetts. Many of those states which have such legislation trumpet this fact in their advertising regarding economic development. In the writer's view, it is probably more important to potential employers, as a kind of ideological litmus test, than as a thing in itself.

Other labor-related legislation of a less general and less well-known nature may be of some import to the economic developer. For example, only New York and Rhode Island pay unemployment-insurance benefits to strikers. As one corporation representative told the writer, in explaining why the firm was thinking of pulling a particular operation out of New York State: "We have branches in many states. When we have a strike, our New York branch is always the last to settle." The law happens to be a red flag to many businessmen, partly because of the reason suggested and partly because of the idea that employers' contributions to the unemployment-insurance fund are actually being used to subsidize strikes. In the case of the firm mentioned above. the writer's organization obtained advantageous tax-exempt financing for it, and the firm, rather than leaving, expanded. Whether the above comments on the law by the firm's spokesman were totally ingenuous, or sprang from a desire to motivate the writer, is known only by the speaker. As in the case of the right-to-work law, one suspects that specific legislation favoring labor or management means more to employers as a sign of political climate than it does strictly for its own sake.

Quality of Life

Though obviously a subjective area, there is no doubt that employers' perceptions of quality of life are important in locational decisions involving activities in which access to raw materials or bulk transportation costs are not major factors. It is particularly true of activities in which ability to recruit specialized personnel is important. In short, it is a major factor in the location of corporate headquarters, many types of service businesses, firms engaged in research and development or other high-technology activities, and in some types of manufacturing other than heavy industry. As noted earlier, improvements in transportation and communication, combined with increased personal income, have made quality-of-life issues more important relative to the more traditional determinants of economic location.

Climate and physical environment are obviously important factors. California's warm air and beaches and Colorado's ski slopes are significant factors in attracting many types of activity. Buffalo's well-publicized record snowstorms two years ago were a discouragement to location in that city. Housing markets within the commuting range of a proposed site may be an important consideration. This is true primarily for the firm which either expects to bring with it many of its present personnel or expects to have to recruit many personnel who are not now area residents.

When office operations are moved, it is common to expect very high attrition rates among secretarial, clerical, and custodial personnel—people who are believed to have commonly found skills and who can be replaced without great disruption to operations. But most companies will make strenuous efforts to keep managerial and technical personnel, part of whose value to the company is their familiarity with its operations. It is at this point that the firm will begin looking at housing markets and asking how much it will cost to relocate personnel to a particular housing market. High prices and long commutes will mean higher wages, bigger relocation costs, and more refusals to be transferred. Similarly, a manufacturer with skilled technical work that cannot be done by the resident labor force will begin to wonder whether or not he can get new workers to move into the area. One force behind the relocation of corporate headquarters from central city to suburb has been the attraction of the suburban housing stock. Objective housing data are available from the decennial census.[9] More current, but less objective impressions, can be had from realtors, tax commissions, assessors, the real estate ads, and finally, direct observation.

The quality of education is a major consideration in relocation for several reasons. One is its implication for labor-force quality. One industrial-location consultant, in a report on the potential market for office space in a major city, wrote the following: "From the businessman's viewpoint, there is considerable doubt that the . . . public high schools are producing the quality of graduates needed to operate modern, sophisticated offices. One-half of all graduates receive general diplomas on completion of their twelfth year, failing to meet qualifications for an academic diploma. As some educators have summarized the problem, students are passed from one grade to the next merely because they have become one year older." [10]

Some of the exodus of firms from central-city locations is explainable in terms of such perceptions as that above. The question, as noted in an earlier chapter, is also wrapped up in the matter of central-city racial and ethnic change.

A second dimension of the question is education for the children of company personnel. A good public-school system is a key recruiting asset. Poor public schools to which middle- and upper-management personnel are reluctant to send their children can be a major discouragement to recruitment. In some cases, managerial personnel may refuse transfer to such locations. In other cases, the cost of private-school tuition may be capitalized in the higher salaries necessary to get personnel to accept transfer. In general, the quality of public education will be well known. If quantitative information is needed, achievement-test scores and other comparative data on school districts can be obtained from state education departments.

The presence of opportunities for higher education is also a powerful consideration in the location of certain types of activity—particularly high-technology firms. The presence of MIT in the Boston area has been a major factor in the ability of that city to attract electronics firms. It is dubious whether the concentration of high-technology firms on route 128 (a circumferential highway around Boston) would exist were it not for the presence of MIT. A considerable number of firms indicated that a factor causing them to locate in the New York suburbs was the existence in New York City of Columbia, New York University, the City University, and other schools at which their people could pursue graduate education.

Public Safety

Fear of crime is a major deterrent to commercial and industrial location. The same consultant's report quoted earlier noted, "Probably no single factor has greater impact on the ability to hold middle-management families . . . than fears relating to security of person and property." Fear of crime takes different forms for different types of activities. For a retailer, it may be primarily that customers will be kept away. For an insurance company, it may be that it will be impossible to recruit women to work on evening shifts. Manufacturing firms located in deteriorating urban areas may find that fear of arson and difficulties in obtaining fire insurance cause them to think seriously about relocating.

In many cases the situation, whether favorable or unfavorable, will be so generally well understood that the economic developer will have no need to do any special research on this subject. If he feels that hard data are needed, some statistics are available from the federal government. [11]

Cost of Living

Indirectly, cost of living affects wage rates (but wage rates can be tracked down directly, as discussed earlier). Directly, however, cost of living will figure in the thinking of prospective firms as it affects their ability to recruit or transfer middle-level managerial and professional personnel. The cost-of-living differences between areas can be quite large. In 1977, the moderate-level budget for a family of four, as computed by the Bureau of Labor Statistics, was $20,609 for Boston and $14,776 for Austin, Texas, to take two extreme cases. Cost-of-living indices for all major metropolitan areas can be obtained from the Bureau of Labor Statistics.[12] For a limited number of metropolitan areas, they can be obtained from the *Statistical Abstract of the United States.*

Commutation and Transportation. This question is of importance mainly in large metropolitan areas.[13] The prospect of a long commute is a discouragement to executive and professional recruitment and also may shorten workweeks. The 9-to-5 office workday in some major cities, in contrast to the 8-to-5 workday in many smaller places, is, in part, a concession to the longer commute. Long commuting times between suburbs and downtown business districts are another reason for the suburbanization of much office activity.

Political Climate

Political climate is another subjective yet important consideration. As the size of the government sector grows, and particularly as the regulatory power of government grows, the political climate as perceived by the would-be industrial or commercial resident becomes increasingly important. The force and flexibility with which land-use controls and environmental controls are applied are often critical. Many firms display a near paranoia on the subject of environmentally based litigation, and there is some substance behind the fears. The firm tied up in litigation regarding, say, a discharge permit or a zoning change watches interest charges and capital costs mount while competitors walk off with former or potential customers. The fact that environmental and public-interest groups often size up the moral high ground adds a dimension of public-relations disaster to many such confrontations. Many firms have a great fear of citizen militancy. A few articulate and well-organized citizens, with a talent for public relations and enough money to afford first-rate legal counsel, can inspire fear in the heart of any corporation president.

Political conservatism is reassuring to many firms because it suggests a generally favorable business attitude and a relative absence of litigation, delay, and confrontation. It cannot be quantified, but it is reasonable to assume and widely believed that the generally more conservative political temper of the South has been an advantage in bidding business away from the more liberal Northeast.

Cost and Availability of Utilities

Electric rates should be compared to the national average and to those in competing locations. The structure of electric rates is complicated for commercial customers, varying with amount consumed, time of consumption, maximum rate of consumption. At this stage, a comparison based on average cost per kilowatt hour to commercial and industrial customers should be sufficient.[14]

Natural-gas availability is an important consideration, for, as noted before, gas presently is substantially less expensive than oil. It is also much less prone to interruption of supply. Gas availability and price can readily be checked with the local utility. For comparative purposes, natural-gas prices can be had from the American Gas Association.[15]

The question of burning coal, which is cheaper, on a BTU basis, than natural gas, is presently so hedged about by environmental constraints and abatement costs that it is not possible to make any sort of simple statement about it. The experience of firms in the area, and consultation with the EPA and state or local environmental agencies would appear to be a logical starting point.

Tax Burden

No complete statement on tax burden is possible since the same tax structure will look different to every firm. No tax has yet been devised that falls equally on all taxpayers. However, some general data should be developed for the area. The two statistics most commonly used for states are total tax burden per capita and taxes as a percentage of total income. A profile of tax burden within the area should also be developed. This includes personal taxes (on income and on personal property), sales taxes, business taxes (on corporate income, capital gains, personal property, inventory). The range of business taxes in the United States is quite large. Taxes in particular areas may include commercial-occupancy, gross-receipts, unincorporated-business taxes.

For interstate comparisons, the *Statistical Abstract of the United States* and the *Census of Governments*, both published by the Bureau of the Census, will provide adequate information. Property taxes per capita and total tax burden for cities and counties can be found in the *County and City Data Book*, another Census Bureau publication. For intrastate purposes, however, the most convenient and comprehensive source in most cases will be the state yearbook or data book. Annual reports by state controllers' offices are also useful.

Land Availability, Land-Use Controls, and Development Costs

For vacant land under existing zoning categories, the best source is often the area's planning agency. Failing that, municipal engineers and assessors are good sources. Zoning, however, should be viewed with a certain sophistication by the economic developer. The reality may or may not be what the map and ordinance indicate. For example, in many suburban areas, a talk with those who have been around the planning scene for some time will reveal that numerous shopping centers, industrial parks, and corporate headquarters now stand on land which was zoned as single-family residential at the time they were proposed. Communities use the device of such zoning to keep land out of development until a fiscally and otherwise attractive proposal is made. At this point, rezoning occurs. Such a strategy also allows the community to bargain with developers over site design and other matters, whereas if land were zoned as commercial in the first instance, construction would take place as a matter of right, without such bargaining. On the other side of the coin, the writer is aware of at least one community in which hundreds of acres without water and sewer connections, and with a generally forbidding topography, are zoned as industrial. The zoning in this case has the effect of providing open space at no municipal cost. Landowners resist residential offers for fear of losing the opportunity of selling to industry at a higher price, but few firms show any interest in locating there.

Finally, in considering land availability, the economic developer should be aware of physical constraints. As a general rule of thumb, commercial construction on slopes over 5 percent (5-foot rise per 100 feet horizontally) is uneconomic. Though in areas where the cost of the best land is very high, construction will occur on steeper slopes, with steepness traded for lower land costs. Remoteness from water and sewer lines is an obstacle to development. Landlocked parcels (without direct road access) may appear in planning-agency land inventories, yet the chance of their being developed may be remote. In recent years, wetland and floodplain zoning has rendered many areas undevelopable.

Thus, any off-the-shelf figure on available land should be tempered with some insight into both land-use control practice and physical reality.

Construction costs relative to other areas can be found in a number of construction handbooks often referred to as "cost calculators."[16] Such books, in addition to having a wealth of material of a technical nature, also have a city-cost index which gives relative costs for major cities. This can be used to make place-to-place comparisons. It can also be used to make rough project estimates. One takes the national cost per square foot given for the type of construction and modifies it by the appropriate city index.

Demographic Characteristics

Demographic characteristics are important to potential firms for various reasons and therefore deserve an initial look by the economic developer. A relatively brief consideration of census data will provide basic statistics, such as population size, labor-force characteristics (percentages of the labor force in various general occupational categories), personal income, educational level of the adult population. To give them some meaning, they should be laid off against the same figures for the state and the nation and for competing local jurisdictions. Much of the data needed are contained in the decennial census.[17]

BEGINNING TO THINK ABOUT STRATEGY

Having reviewed the area characteristics, whether in a formal and structured way or otherwise, a logical next step is to begin thinking about how broad categories of economic activity and the area are suited to each other.

Categories to be discussed here are retailing, wholesaling and related operations, corporate headquarters, other large-office functions, research and development, business services, personal services, and manufacturing. Left out of this list are agriculture, extractive industries, and other activities tied to particular physical resources, terrain, or climatic features.

The predominant determinant of retailing location is demographic characteristics. Large retailers are among the most sophisticated business users of demographic data. Large retailing chains will often have on their staffs economists, statisticians, or others skilled in manipulating demographic data, estimating market shares, projecting population growth. Smaller retailers are also very much motivated by demographic characteristics, though obviously their resources for manipulating data are not the same. Once the general choice of area is made, the next determinant is access or traffic flow. In big-city central business districts, pedestrian traffic flow may be the most important variable. In Manhattan, where the pattern is a grid of streets running east/west and of avenues running north/south, store rentals on avenues are substantially greater than on the streets because avenues have heavier pedestrian traffic. Proximity to a subway stop is capitalized in higher rents because of greater pedestrian traffic. In less densely developed areas, it is vehicular rather than pedestrian traffic that is paramount.

In terms of assessing whether or not substantial amounts of retailing can be attracted, the place to start is with demographic characteristics, particularly personal income. The second question is whether there exists unsatisfied demand. Whether a net retail outflow exists can generally be determined from a combination of formal and informal sources. On the formal side, *Census of Retailing* statistics can be laid off against income and population statistics from the decennial census.[18] This will indicate whether the ratio of retail sales to personal income is lower or higher than the state or metropolitan average. A lower-than-average ratio suggests net outflow. These numerical estimates can be supplemented by observations of shopper behavior, whether from surveys or casual inquiry. Here, the economic developer and the prospective retailer may have somewhat different perspectives. Unless there is some net outflow to be stopped, or there are outside sales to be captured, the economic developer may regard bringing in additional activity as playing a zero sum game. The retailer, however, will naturally take a competitive rather than an aggregate view of the situation.

The other area characteristics mentioned earlier, such as tax burden, wage rates, labor-force quality, are likely to weigh quite lightly with the retailer as compared to demand and physical access.

Wholesaler location is partly dependent upon the presence of retailers. Therefore, in the growth process, the movement in of retailers often precedes the movement in of wholesalers. When a certain threshold is reached, wholesaling growth may be very rapid. Good access for trucking is a major, if not the single most important, determinant of location for wholesalers. Neighborhood appearance and visibility are generally not important. Wholesaler location may be highly sensitive to land costs because warehouses, on a per-square-foot basis, are one of the least expensive forms of construction. Thus, land costs represent a higher percentage of the total cost. If zoning and other land-use controls mandate large setbacks or low coverage ratios for distributive activities, the sensitivity to land costs will be further increased.

Corporate headquarters are, in several ways, unique entities so far as locational choice is concerned. Questions of image and prestige play a larger role than in the location of any other type of activity.

Accessibility is a key determining item. In past years this decreed central business district locations. In the age of the automobile and the limited-access highway, most headquarters construction has been in the ring around the central city. The preferred combination for many is a bucolic-appearing site very close to the interchange of a major limited-access route. Air transportation appears to be regarded as a necessity for many corporate headquarters. In some cases, access to an airport with good scheduled services is considered adequate. In other cases, proximity to a general-aviation airport capable of handling corporate aircraft is required. The complex of issues previously discussed under the heading of quality of life appears to be important. This relates in part to the corporate-image question and in part to the matter of middle-management attraction and retention. Most corporate headquarters have substantial secretarial and clerical needs, so that labor-force availability is a significant factor. Closeness to business services appears to be important in inverse relationship to headquarters size. Not surprisingly, the large headquarters will internalize services that others contract out for, and will thus be more independent in this regard. Land costs, construction costs, local taxes, and even wage rates do not appear to weigh as heavily as with many types of activity. This may be in part because the headquarters is overhead and is not treated as a profit center, as are other operations.

For other types of office activity, questions of prestige and image are likely to be less important. If the work is of a more routinized nature, such as processing insurance claims and policies, much less interaction with the outside world is required. Labor-force availability and quality, and wage rates are likely to be the most important locational factors. Utility and energy costs will probably be relatively minor considerations because they represent a very small fraction of total operating expense. A typical cost for utilities for a modern office building might be $1 per square foot per year. With, say, one worker per 300 gross square feet (a common figure), a variation of 25 percent from that ratio would result in a cost differential of $75 per worker per year, probably less than one half of 1 percent of annual operating expense.

Research and development activities, in general, locate largely on the basis of labor-force availability and the opportunity for useful interaction with firms or organizations in related activities. Attractive climate, presence of recreational and cultural facilities, presence of major educational institutions, and presence of firms doing related work seem to be the dominant considerations. Being close to firms engaged in similar efforts does entail the risks of losing key personnel through piracy and the leakage of proprietary information to competitors, but it also offers corresponding advantages along these same lines. More generally, there is likely to be a synergistic effect for everyone. The firm which is remote from a center of activity is likely to suffer from being out of touch. More traditional considerations, such as transportation costs, land costs, tax structure, and even wage rates, are likely to be much less important. A recent campaign to attract electronics firms from California's "Silicon Valley" to suburban Maryland outside of Washington, D.C., is based heavily upon the existence of a superior professional- and technical-labor supply around Washington. The argument is that the presence of consultants, federal agencies, research and development organizations, and think tanks has built up an almost unmatched concentration of specialized and highly qualified manpower. It is thus availability, rather than cost, which the campaign stresses.

In general, business services are highly market oriented. Like retailing, the prime locational determinant is likely to be the presence of potential customers. Locations which minimize personnel travel costs, both for the firm and for customers, are highly favored. As in retailing, all considerations other than market access are likely to play a relatively small role. Matters of image and prestige of location may or may not play a significant role, depending upon the type of service.

Much the same comments can be made for personal services. Access to customers and by customers is the predominant consideration. Whether or not image and prestige considerations affect location will be a function of the type of service.

Manufacturing is difficult to generalize about. Some types of manufacturing are tied to sources of raw materials. Processes in which there is a fairly low value per ton of product are particularly sensitive to transportation costs. If the process is weight losing (steelmaking was given as an example earlier), it is often located closer to raw materials to minimize transportation costs. Processes in which weight is gained in the final production stages (soda bottling is a common example) are often located close to customers, as are firms which produce a product which is perishable in one sense or another (bakery products, daily-newspaper printing).

In light manufacturing, much industry is said to be "footloose." If a product is sold to a national or a large regional market, does not require specialized labor pools, and is not tied to sources of raw materials, the industry may product is sold to a national or a large regional market, does not require specialized labor pools, and is not tied to sources of raw materials, the industry may have a tremendous choice in location. Labor costs, land costs, construction costs, tax rates, and financing assistance may thus prove to be the determining locational factors. Much of the industrial growth of the South in recent years has resulted from its ability to attract and encourage the growth of footloose industry. The ability to utilize a relatively unspecialized labor force is a major requirement for the quality of footlooseness. For example, much of New York City's garment industry has been lost to the Southeast, and some of it to areas outside the United States, such as the Caribbean. The most skilled activities, however, have tended to remain in the city. More than anything else, labor-skill requirements seem to have been the determining factor enabling firms to leave. Activities like fine jewelry making and diamond cutting appear to have remained in the city because of their specialized labor requirements.

Utility requirements and energy costs have different effects, depending upon the nature of the manufacturing operation. The cost of electric power may be a minor item for a firm engaged in sheet-metal fabrication, but is a critical one for firms engaged in die casting or injection molding, where electric power is used to melt materials prior to working.

ANALYSIS OF RECENT TRENDS

After making a preliminary reconnaissance of the area and giving some thought to the types of activity most and least suited to the area, it is well to look at recent trends to see whether events are occurring as expected. If they are, it suggests that the economic developer's perceptions of the area are accurate. If they are not, rethinking of the situation may be advisable. Very often, a disparity between what is happening and what ought to happen will be a source of further insight into the area.

As an example of matching what is happening with what ought to be happening, the following quick sketch of a county in the New York suburbs is provided:

• wage rates typical of the entire New York area, i.e., typical of metropolitan areas but higher than most nonmetropolitan areas;

• a labor force with higher-than-average educational attainment and a heavy concentration in professional and technical, and secretarial and clerical occupations;

• a generally high rating for many quality-of-life issues, including public education, attractive physical environment, proximity to various cultural and recreational activities;

• high land costs, tight environmental regulations, and generally restrictive land-use controls;

• excellent highway access to the New York/New England region;
• site of one of the three major general-aviation airports in the metropolitan area;
• high property taxes, high personal taxes (characteristic of New York State), moderately high business taxes;
• proximity to New York City and good highway and rail links to the Manhattan central business district;
• the highest electric-power costs in the continental United States.
• well-above-average (for both the state and nation) levels of family income;
• low rates of residential construction and extremely tight housing markets.

The economic picture was as follows:

• rapid losses of manufacturing production jobs (about one-third of all such jobs were lost from the late 1960s to the mid-1970s);
• rapid growth in corporate-headquarters activity;
• rapid growth in retailing and personal services;
• blue-collar unemployment rates that were about twice white-collar unemployment rates;
• high levels of welfare dependence among the minority population;
• high levels of female labor-force participation;
• generally optimistic views on the local economy expressed by bankers, corporate executives, and retailers; generally pessimistic views on the local economy expressed by manufacturers, union leaders, and the construction industry.

The above summary could be elaborated on at considerable length. But taking it at face value, a basic consistency is evident.

Considerations of labor-force quality and availability, quality of life, accessibility, and proximity to a major city made the county highly attractive to corporate-headquarters, research and development, and related activities. The high female labor-force participation rates were partly a function of the very large number of secretarial and clerical jobs offered by headquarters operations. The high levels of family income had several sources: job mix, with a large proportion of well-paying corporate jobs; the high female labor-force participation rates (meaning many two-income families); and the proximity of New York City, offering a large number of technical, professional, and managerial jobs to county residents.

The loss of manufacturing jobs was consistent with high power costs, high land costs, high property taxes, tight land-use controls, and wage rates exceeding those of nonmetropolitan areas. The pattern of unemployment was consistent with a pattern of job change that tightened white-collar markets while softening blue-collar markets. The high level of minority dependence on welfare was consistent with the movement of the economy in a direction which demanded white-collar skills not possessed by many members of the minority community.

To get a quick picture of what has been happening in the area's economy in the last several years, a number of standard sources are generally available. The single most useful statistic, and one that is usually immediately available, is employment by major sector. For cities and counties, these data are usually available, on a monthly or quarterly basis, from the state labor department and, in some cases, from regional planning agencies. A common breakdown of employment by major industry is as follows: manufacturing; trade (retailing and wholesaling); construction; finance, insurance, and real estate; agriculture; mining and extractive industries; government and public-education services; miscellaneous.

Two cautions are to be noted. First, some sources give employment by place of work and others, by place of residence. Where the area is a natural economic unit, the two figures will be roughly the same, but where the area is only part of a natural economic area—for example, a city which is part of a larger metropolitan area—the figures may be substantially different. Second, such categories as those above describe the industry of employment, and not what types of work are actually performed. This is particularly misleading in the case of manufacturing. Most of the "manufacturing" workers in Gary, Indiana, are actually production workers. Most of the "manufacturing" workers in Fairfield County, Connecticut are office workers; the county contains a large number of corporate headquarters and relatively few production facilities.

The unemployment rate is a second readily available statistic. For most cities and counties, it can be had on a monthly or quarterly basis, from the state labor department. Unemployment data from the census are available only once a decade. They may be useful, however, for furnishing a baseline for various calculations. For some cities and counties, unemployment statistics may be available by occupation of worker or by race of worker. These figures are generally less reliable than the overall unemployment figures, but may still serve to provide some insight. Even if unemployment rates by occupation of worker are not directly available, they often can be inferred, without much effort from other data sources. For example, many state labor departments or state employment agencies maintain information on the occupation of unemployment-insurance recipients. When the occupation of unemployment recipients is compared with the data about the occupation of all residents, rough estimates of relative unemployment rates can be made. In the suburban county mentioned ealier, there were roughly two white-collar workers for each blue-collar worker, yet the number of unemployment recipients from the two groups was roughly equal. Thus. if the overall rate were 6 percent, white-collar unemplooyment was estimated at 4.5 percent and blue-collar unemployment at 9 percent. This simple finding was consistent with employment trends that showed the area losing construction and manufacturing production jobs while gaining employment in government, business services, and retailing. It furnished one of the bases for determining that economic development efforts should emphasize the attraction and retention of distribution and light-manufacturing production operations.

Labor-force participation rates may also provide insight into the general movement of the economy. These rates are available once a decade from the decennial census. In the intervening years, they can be estimated by comparing employment data with current population estimates.

Property-tax rolls furnish a useful source of data that is generally available with little effort. Most major municipalities have summarized assessment data that can provide quick insight into trends in commercial construction. Generally speaking, summarized data are available for residential and commercial structures, amd within the latter, several categories of structures are provided. As a note of caution, one should be clear about what changes in the numbers mean. For example, assume that one sees a steady increase in the value of factories and warehouses. This may be because the municipality assesses on a full-value basis and readjusts values each year for changes in estimated market price. In this case, one must ascertain what adjustments have been made, before reaching conclusions about the real magnitude of change in this category. On the other hand, the community may adjust assessments only infrequently and deal with the question of changing market value by adjusting its equalization rate annually.[19] In this case, it may be possible to use assessment data without adjustment.

Changes in the rate at which the tax base is growing in different categories may provide a sort of leading indicator of economic trends. If manufacturing employment is rising but no industrial construction is taking place, the rise may simply be a reflection of the uptrend in the business cycle nationally, while the lack of investor confidence points to a problem in the future.

An alternative to assessment data is building-permit data. In one way, the latter are superior in that they are available sooner; permits are filed before construction begins, whereas properties do not appear on the tax rolls until completed. For the developer whose jurisdiction is a single municipality, that place itself is usually the best source of permit data. If the developer's responsibility includes a large number of jurisdictions, it may be easier to get usable data from a higher level of government.

To track recent population changes, the economic developer can make use of the Bureau of the Census, which makes indirect estimates of the population and per capita income. These are made for every municipality in the United States every year (and data lag behind by about two years).[20]

NOTES

1. There is a large body of location theory, developed over many years and presented by a number of writers, including William Alonso, Walter Isaard, August Losch. Much of it is quite elegant mathematically, and its use requires a substantial amount of staff time and technical sophistication. In this writer's view, elaborate studies of accessibility are not cost effective for most development agencies. For more formal approaches to accessibility, see

Barry M. Moriarty and David J. Cowen, eds., *Industrial Location and Community Development*, University of North Carolina Press, Chapel Hill, 1980. A practical grasp of the rudiments of location may be helpful. See William Alonso, "Location Theory," in *Regional Development and Planning: A Reader*, John Friedman and William Alonso, eds., MIT Press, Cambridge, Mass., 1964. The same article can also be found in *Readings in Urban Economics*, Matthew Edel and Jerome Rothenberg, eds., Macmillan, New York, 1972.

2. *Transportation Energy Conservation Data Book*, A. S. Loebl et al., Oak Ridge National Laboratory (reprinted by National Technical Information Service, U.S. Dept. of Commerce), 1976.

3. Obviously the priority given to various factors will differ by industry, and not all studies will show an identical ranking of the importance of various locational factors. For a review of a number of studies and citations of the literature, see George A. Reigeluth and Hal Wolman, "The Determinants and Implications of Communities' Changing Competitive Advantages: A Review of Literature," working paper 1264-03, Urban Institute, Washington, D.C., 1979.

4. Bureau of Labor Statistics, Area Wage Surveys, U.S. Dept. of Labor, Washington, D.C. In general, labor-market areas are surveyed on a three-year cycle, with different places surveyed at different points in the cycle. Thus, some standardizing has to be done to get data for comparable places surveyed at different times.

5. Bureau of Labor Statistics, *Employment and Earnings*, U.S. Dept. of Labor, Washington, D.C.

6. In the 1970 census, these data items appeared in *Characteristics of the Population*. The most detailed tabulations are at state and SMSA levels. However, a substantial amount of data are also available at the county and municipality levels. In SMSAs, a number of labor-force data items are available at the census-tract level as well.

7. These are generally available at the county and large-municipality levels, from state labor departments. At the state and major labor-market area levels, they can be obtained from *Employment and Earnings* as well.

8. Some caution should be advised here. As a rule of thumb, recipients are about half of the total unemployed and may not represent an entirely random sample of the unemployed. This may be especially true in periods of prolonged unemployment when some of the unemployed exhaust their benefits and drop off the list of recipients without leaving the ranks of the unemployed.

9. Bureau of the Census, *Census of Housing*, U.S. Dept. of Commerce, Washington, D.C.

10. Survey taken by Westchester County Dept. of Planning, Spring 1969.

11. Uniform statistics on a variety of offenses are available from the Federal Bureau of Investigation, Washington, D.C.

12. Bureau of Labor Statistics, Dept. of Labor, *Urban Family Budgets and Comparative Indexes for Selected Urban Areas* (Annual), Washington, D.C.

13. Data are available, on a decennial basis, in both *Characteristics of the Population* and *Journey to Work*, Bureau of the Census, Dept. of Commerce, Washington, D.C.

14. U.S. Federal Power Commission, *Rate Series*, Washington, D.C.

15. American Gas Association, Arlington, Va., *Gas Facts Annual.*

16. *Means Construction Indexes*, R.S. Means Co., Duxbury, Mass., and *Dodge Building Cost Calculator and Valuation Guide*, McGraw Hill Book Co., New York.

17. *Characteristics of the Population*, op. cit.

18. *The Census of Retailing* is taken in years ending in 2 and 7, so that some statistical adjustments are necessary to relate its findings to the income data of the decennial census. If the jurisdiction has a sales tax, annual totals will provide a good index of the rate of change in retail sales.

19. This is a rate which is applied to the assessed value of property to convert it to full value. It is similar in principle to the assessment ratio.

20. Bureau of the Census, U.S. Dept. of Commerce, *Current Population Reports*, Series P 25, Washington, D.C.

7

DEVELOPMENT PLANNING

Few economic developers will be called upon to do detailed site planning. That is work done most commonly by planning or engineering consultants. However, the economic developer sometimes does, and more often should, participate in the community's overall planning process. This chapter is provided as background for such participation.

A primary goal of the economic developer is to assure that an adequate supply of land is set aside for industrial and commercial development in the fore-seeable future. It is also important to assure that land-use controls are reasonable and that land-use plans do not contain within them the seeds of future opposition to commercial and industrial development.

ESTIMATING LAND NEEDS

One place to begin thinking about industrial and commercial land-use needs is with the floor-space requirements per worker for different types of activity. From such figures, acreage requirements for likely levels of employment can be estimated. Such estimates are necessarily rough ones, but can still be highly useful for planning purposes. Table 7.1 shows figures which can be used as starting points.

These figures are guidelines only and large variations may occur within categories. For example, electronics assembly or garment manufacturing, where the product is not bulky and workers sit almost shoulder to shoulder, might

TABLE 7.1

Gross Floor-Space Requirements

Activity	Gross Square Footage per Employee
Retailing	500
Wholesaling and warehousing	1,000
Light manufacturing	500
Heavy manufacturing	1,000
Office activities	250
Research and development	500

Sources: Joseph D. Chiara and Lee Koppleman, *Planning Design Criteria*, Van Nostrand & Reinhold, New York, 1969; Donald C. Lochmoeller et al., *Industrial Development Handbook*, Urban Land Institute, Washington, D.C., 1975; Travel and Facilities Section, Transportation Planning Division, Arizona Dept. of Transportation, in cooperation with U.S. Dept. of Transportation, *Trip Generation Intensity Factors*, Federal Highway Administration, 1976; John M. Levy et al., *Commercial and Public Construction in Westchester County*, Westchester County Dept. of Planning, White Plains, N.Y., 1974.

average under 200 square feet per worker, while assembly of sheet-metal ductwork for heating and air-conditioning systems might average well over 500 square feet per worker. Yet all fall in the light-manufacturing category.

The coverage ratio—the ratio between floor area and land area—is subject to considerable variation due to differences in degree of urbanization, land costs, and land-use controls. A substantial percentage of commercially used land is devoted to parking. Here, too, variations are great, depending upon the same variables listed above as well as upon the availability of public transportation. A parking-area-to-floor-area ratio adequate for a downtown department store might spell economic disaster for a suburban shopping center five miles away.

As an example of estimating work force per acre, consider light manufacturing in an industrial-park setting in a suburban or nonmetropolitan area. One-story construction is assumed. Where land values are low, the one-story manufacturing structure is favored for a number of reasons. Lighter construction is possible. Interior space is not lost to stairwells and elevator shafts. Materials handling is often more efficient and the layout is more amenable to straight-through processes. If an area is not highly urbanized, most of the work force will arrive by car. An allowance of 0.8 parking spaces per employee would be reasonable. Typically, parking areas without parking attendants require 350 to 400 square feet per car, about half for spaces and half for circulation. If we allow 500 square feet of floor space per worker, total land coverage per worker is now up to about 800 square feet. If a reasonable allowance is made for truck loading and visitor parking, this figure might rise to 1,000 square feet. Not all of an industrial-park site can be used. Land-use controls will call for some buffering space. Topographic, drainage, or other physical problems may further reduce usable area. If we assume, somewhat conservatively, that only 50 percent of the average industrial-park site will be usable, then the land area per worker rises to 2,000 square feet, yielding a figure of 22 workers per acre.

There is obviously no way to predict employee density precisely, but the figure will serve for rough planning purposes. Comparable calculations can be made for other types of activity. For corporate headquarters in the suburbs, employee density might be placed at one worker per 300 gross square feet and parking requirements at three spaces per 1,000 square feet. Assuming a one-story structure and no structured parking, about 600 square feet per worker are required for floor space and parking area. Assuming 50 percent site utilization, this would suggest about 36 workers per acre.

Since parking requirements are a major factor in land requirements, standards for a number of types of activity are shown in Table 7.2. Note that these are all given for situations in which space is not a major constraint. High densities of development, the existence of heavily utilized public transportation, and high land costs will all force these figures down. As land costs rise from being measured in cents per square foot to dollars per square foot, multistory construction becomes economical for many types of commercial use. Where land costs surpass, say, $500,000 per acre, parking structures may become economical.[1]

TABLE 7.2

Parking Requirements for Various Types of Activity

Activity	Spaces per 1,000 Gross Square Feet*
Light manufacturing	2
Heavy industry	1
Corporate headquarters and other office activities	3
Wholesaling and warehousing	1
Regional shopping center	4
Neighborhood shopping center	2

*Assumes suburban density of development and relatively low utilization of public transportation.

Sources: Joseph D. Chiara and Lee Koppleman, *Planning Design Criteria*, Van Nostrand & Reinhold, New York, 1969, and Donald C. Lochmoeller et al., *Industrial Development Handbook*, Urban Land Institute, Washington, D.C., 1975.

Observations and estimates are by the author.

In estimating land requirements per worker, several cautions should be observed. In general, it is best to make assumptions on the basis of recent density of development. Observe what has been done and sold recently; no better guide to marketability can be found. Do not lean too heavily on existing zoning ordinances in making such estimates. Where zoning specifies unrealistically low densities, the economic forces for rezoning and/or the granting of variances are very powerful. So, too, may be the legal forces. On the other hand, zoning ordinance may, on occasion, permit densities of development that practice and technology will not sustain. Zoning puts a ceiling on density, but does not compel construction at that density. For example, assume a zoning ordinance in a suburban area specifies a maximum floor-area ratio (FAR) of 0.8 for light manufacturing. The chances that anyone will build to this density are remote. There is, as noted above, a strong preference for single-story plants. Parking, circulation, and truck-unloading space will probably require as much square footage per worker as will the building itself. We are thus down to an FAR of .5 already. Given some loss of space for buffering and setback requirements, the probable FAR drops still further. In modern suburban light-manufacturing development, an FAR of .2 or .3 is a reasonable estimate. It is rare that any sizable area develops to the maximum permitted by zoning.

Do not expect new development to be more dense than existing development unless there is some convincing reason for it that can be pointed to. Thirty years ago, there were four Americans for every automobile. There are now about two Americans per automobile. This alone should make one wary of expecting new development to be denser than the average for the present inventory.

It should also be understood that not all land apparently available for development will be developed. Initial development may leave behind parcels of small size or unsuitable geometry. Environmental or other unanticipated problems may arise. The market for industrial and commercial space may change. In short, space requirements should be estimated realistically and generously.

At the risk of saying the obvious, it is important to avoid wishful thinking. For reasons ranging from air quality to the balance of payments, it would be desirable if the U.S. population made a major shift from the single-occupant auto to car pooling and public transportation. Some shift in that direction appears to be occurring. But to assume that it will be sufficient to radically alter the market for commercial land, and then to proceed on that basis, would be quite risky.

Beyond simply assuring adequate acreage, some specific points need to be considered:

● Development cost rises with steepness of grade. As a rule of thumb, slopes over 5 percent should be regarded as relatively unlikely to be developed. (In urban areas, one can find both residential and commercial development on much steeper slopes. But this is often a residual from the days when a different transportation technology and land-use pattern placed a much greater emphasis on centrality.) Industrial land should be well drained and relatively free of major obstacles to construction, for example, rock outcroppings, and should be outside the flood plain. It should also not be located so that its development poses significant environmental problems. If it does, community opposition and litigation can be anticipated when the time for development approaches.

• Availability of utilities is an obvious consideration. Water, sewer, and adequate electric service are vital. Natural gas, at this writing, costs little more than half as much, per BTU, as oil and thus is highly desirable.

• Adequate access is essential. What constitutes adequate access varies by industry. For corporate headquarters, automobile access is primary. For a wholesaler, being close to a good truck route is likely to be the predominant consideration. Some manufacturers will be concerned only with highway access. Others will regard rail access as being desirable or essential.

In many instances, it is desirable to achieve some separation between commercial and other traffic for the sake of minimizing community opposition to development. Additional traffic is often the number-one reason for community opposition to commercial and industrial development. The writer witnessed the sudden death of an industrial-park proposal in a community which needed it very badly. It became apparent to the politically popular legislator of an adjacent community that a small number of trucks would travel for several hundred yards through a lightly populated part of her community. The objection seemed trivial to the writer and a number of others, but overwhelming to the legislator. The site has been growing weeds ever since.

Future traffic capacity is also a factor to be considered. In general, one cannot expect a community to pay for lane miles of roadway years in advance of the time they will be needed. On the other hand, traffic generation from industrially and commercially zoned land can be estimated and rights of way can be reserved. Peak-hour volumes (the critical figure in most cases) can be estimated. For most agglomerations of activities, the peak hours are the morning and evening rush hour, with volume in the evening peak generally somewhat higher. For particular activities, however, the peak hour may not coincide with the general peak. For example, the retailing peak hour generally occurs in the afternoon before the evening rush hour begins. Table 7.3 shows average peak-hour/trip-generation figures for a number of activities. Much more detailed information can be obtained from the traffic-engineering literature, including the document cited in Table 7.3.

The reader will note the ratios between the per-employee and the per-1,000-square-feet figures have implicit in them floor space per worker and that these implicit figures correspond approximately to those of Table 7.1.

From peak-hour figures, the adequacy of the existing or proposed road network can be estimated. Making such estimates is a technical matter best left to the traffic engineer. To provide a rough number for thinking about capacity, a

TABLE 7.3

Peak-Hour Trip Generation for Various Types of Activities

Activity	1,000 Gross Sq. Ft.	Peak-Hour Trips by Employee
Industrial parks	.8	.5
Large shopping centers	2.3	1.1
Offices	2.5	.6
Warehouses	1.0	.9
Large free-standing factories	.8	.4
Small free-standing factories	1.2	.5
Research and development facilities	1.2	.6

Source: Travel and Facilities Section, Transportation Planning Division, Arizona Dept. of Transportation, in cooperation with U.S. Dept. of Transportation, *Trip Generation Intensity Factors*, Federal Highway Administration, Washington, D.C., 1976.

modern freeway, under ideal conditions, might achieve a volume of 2,000 cars per lane per hour.[2] Frequent interchanges, grades, curves, reduced sight distances, and trucking all lower this figure. In general, a two-way, two-lane road, with passing permitted in both directions, has no more total capacity than a single comparable lane in one direction would have. Intersections reduce roadway capacity as do merging or exiting points. Strip development reduces highway capacity in the latter manner. One might think of it as introducing turbulence into the traffic stream, much as scale inside a pipe introduces turbulence into the flow of water.

It would be naïve to argue that adequate road capacity must always be present for development to occur. In many cases the congestion caused by development provides the pressure to increase road capacity. Then, too, there is often more give in the system than initial estimates suggest. For example, when peak-hour congestion becomes a serious problem, firms may begin staggering work hours. In addition, some nonbusiness traffic may be shifted to nonpeak hours. A road which is at capacity in the peak hour may accommodate still more traffic as congestion spreads the peak over more time. Nonetheless, to the extent possible, it is worthwhile for the economic developer to press the case for providing adequate capacity. If nothing else, he can urge that the option to provide future capacity not be foreclosed. Congestion costs are a major deterrent to attracting industry. But beyond this direct effort, congestion generates an anti-development, anti-growth sentiment.

The importance of access by public transportation is a somewhat cloudy matter. As noted earlier, a rebirth of public transportation in the United States is widely hoped for and perhaps not quite so widely anticipated. Whether it will occur remains to be seen. At the bottom of the issue may be future energy availability, a matter upon which there is sharp disagreement among experts.[3] At present, about 6 percent of the U.S. labor force gets to work by public transportation.[4] Public transportation has the greatest chances for success when the collection and distribution problems are minimized by high residential densities in one area and high employment densities in another. The trend in land use in the last several decades has clearly made both of these problems more severe in most parts of the United States. When population densities fall below several thousand per square mile, the collection problem can become overwhelming. Perhaps the best one can say on this point is to urge the economic developer to think realistically on the subject, to avoid confusing what should happen with what will happen, and to hedge his bets as much as possible.

Site Geometry

A parcel 250 feet by 1,600 feet holds far less industrial potential than a parcel 500 feet by 800 feet, when all other conditions are equal. The latter parcel can be developed with fewer feet of internal roadway and less expenditure on utility lines; it has a shorter periphery, which minimizes land lost for buffering and setbacks. The greater depth will permit building and loading-area shapes that cannot be accommodated on the shallower parcel. Thus, a land inventory composed of many small or oddly shaped pieces may hold a great deal less potential than the simple addition of acreage will suggest. Large blocks of land with sufficient depth are highly desirable. Industry requirements vary tremendously. Chapin and Kaiser quote 1,000 feet as a desirable minimum depth for a rail-served site (the ideal configuration being a site located between parallel rail and highway rights of way). This is essentially a heavy-industry criterion, as indicated by the term "rail served." For highway-served sites (generally meaning light industry), they quote a minimum depth of 600-to-800 feet.[5] These numbers are not binding and one can see successful development in many urban areas where they are not met. Nonetheless, if they can be achieved, the chance of seeing development take place is enhanced.

SEPARATION OF USES

Since the inception of zoning about the time of World War I, it has been understood that residential areas should be protected from industry for obvious and unarguable reasons.[6] It took several decades to realize that there are strong, though less obvious reasons for seeking to exclude residential uses from industrial areas.

One reason is to prevent the breakup of large parcels. Large parcels can always be subdivided for small industrial and commercial users if that is what market forces dictate. However, if large parcels are broken up by scattered residential development, some industrial and commercial opportunities are permanently lost. But perhaps a more important reason for the prohibition of residential development in commercial and industrial zones is a political one. By permitting residential development (or some types of public development) in a commercial or industrial zone, a predictably antidevelopment constituency is created. The fact that someone buys or rents a house in an area, knowing its predominant zoning is industrial, does not prevent him from opposing subsequent development on the grounds that it intrudes upon his tranquility or lowers the value of his investment. This phenomenon has been noted, in particular, in connection with airports. Populations which have moved in after the airport was in operation have often exerted strenuous pressures to reduce or at least block the expansion of airport activity. Rather than becoming involved in after-the-fact conflict, it is better to avoid conflict by zoning in such a manner that the problem does not arise.

Reasonableness in zoning is, of course, a term that cannot be defined precisely. To the writer, it implies some compromise between the needs of commerce and industry on one hand and legitimate community goals on the other. The writer tends to favor performance standards over rigid categories, as do many planners. Rather than zoning out warehousing because it may involve excessive truck traffic, why not define permitted uses in terms of vehicle trips? Rather than banning machine shops because of their potential for noise, why not cast part of the ordinance in terms of decibels?

In adopting an ordinance, it is very easy to include requirements which do not confer great benefits on the community but do impose substantial costs on users. Many, if not most, zoning ordinances are adaptations of other ordinances. Few are written de novo. The planning consultant who turns out zoning ordinances for client communities is likely to do a certain amount on an off-the-shelf basis and realize some economies of scale in their production. Then, too, there is often a tendency to lean in the direction of restrictiveness simply because it is to the community that the draft ordinance is submitted for approval. Because the land-value reduction caused by zoning is not a cost borne by the community, there is little motivation to ascertain that the public benefits equal the private costs.

For example, an unduly low coverage requirement may make some types of commercial development uneconomic. Assume that commercially zoned land sells for $1 a square foot (not an unreasonably high figure in many metropolitan areas). If the maximum coverage permitted for warehousing is lowered from 40 percent to 20 percent, the land cost per square foot of building rises from $2.50 to $5.00. A typical construction cost for warehouses in the United States (in 1980) is about $15 per gross square foot.[7] In effect, the changed coverage requirement is equivalent to a 16 percent increase in construction cost—quite possibly a figure sufficient to move the activity to a competing community.

If the lower coverage requirement really serves community purposes, then perhaps it is worth the lost tax revenues and jobs. But because the act of zoning itself costs the municipality nothing, one should make an effort to see that the zoning process does not achieve small community benefits at the price of large, but not immediately evident community or private costs.[8] Similar comments might be made with regard to other aspects of zoning, such as setback and screening requirements, parking requirements, height and bulk requirements, lists of permitted and nonpermitted uses. The question is whether requirements meet real community needs (which they often do), or whether some of them are there because they are in the ordinance from which the later ordinance was copied, or in a more general sense, because they have no explicit cost to the community.

Particularly in suburban areas, there often is a community preference for low coverage ratios (low FARs). This is understandable because low ratios imply smaller impacts upon both the particular parcel of land itself and the immediate environs. There may, however, be a price to be paid at least in two respects. First, there may result a more scattered pattern of development that generates increased vehicular traffic and eats up potential open space. Site impact is minimized but community or regional impact is not. Second, there is the possibility that where usable commercial land is limited, excessive coverage requirements will exact a price from the community later on. The corporate headquarters which employs 1,200 on a 100-acre tract with an FAR of 0.07 (calculated from a ratio of 250 gross square feet per employee) may be extremely attractive to the community.[9] It offers a revenue/cost surplus and preserves a substantial amount of green space at no public cost. In the long term, however, the exchange of a very large block of prime commercial land for a relatively small number of jobs may be regretted.

In the writer's decade in planning and economic development, he has never heard a community object to industrial or commercial development on the grounds of not being dense enough. But if developable land, in sufficiently large parcels with suitable geometry, is one of the community's prime economic assets, perhaps this apparently inevitable preference for low density is a form of municipal myopia.

In 1951 the National Industrial Zoning Committee established 11 principles of industrial zoning, which are worth quoting here:[10]

1. Most communities require a certain amount of industrial development to produce a sound economy.
2. Zoning controls are basic tools in the reservation of space for industry; guidance of industrial location into a desirable pattern; and, provision of related facilities and areas needed for convenient and balanced economy.

3. Industrial use is a legitimate land use possessing integrity comparable to other classes of land use established under zoning and is entitled to protection against encroachment.
4. Through proper zoning, industrial and residential areas can be good neighbors.
5. Industry will continue to grow and most industries will require larger areas in the future. There is need for a reclassification of industry based on modern manufacturing processes and the prevailing policy of plant construction in order to determine the desirability for inclusion in a given area.
6. Industrial potentialities of lands bearing a favorable relationship to transportation should be recognized in the zoning process.
7. Industrial zoning and highway planning should go hand in hand.
8. Special consideration should be given to the street layout in industrial areas.
9. Zoning ordinances should be permissive rather than prohibitive.
10. A good zoning ordinance should be sufficiently definite to convey to a landowner a clear concept of what he can do with his land.
11. Industrial zoning can be most effective when considered on a metropolitan basis.

Perhaps the most difficult question is how much land to reserve for industrial and commercial use. Koppleman and Chiara suggest planning for a 50-year horizon, but obviously any number one might name is an arbitrary figure.[11] How much employment growth to expect within a given period is another question. If there is some consensus about the future of population growth, inferences can then be made regarding employment. Nationally, there are about 45 people in the work force for every 100 of population, a ratio which is probably good enough for rough approximations. But it must be noted that population projection is far from a science. Looking at old population estimates in the light of current data is not usually a confidence-inspiring experience.

It must be emphasized that land requirements should be estimated reasonably generously, for, almost inevitably, a certain amount of land reserved for commercial and industrial uses will not be used for such purposes, for reasons noted earlier. It should also be noted that the overall direction in the demand for industrial and commercial land has changed before and may well change again. For much of this century, the demand for land in central places weakened relative to the demand in peripheral locations. Industrial land values and space rentals in urban areas fell relative to those in suburban and nonmetropolitan places. Rail access and water access fell in importance relative to road access. For many types of activity, accessibility by public transportation declined in importance. Whether these trends will be reversed or continue remains to be seen.

Energy costs may be a key to the issue but, given the divergence in expert opinion on the future of energy costs, it would be foolish to hazard a guess as to whether they will rise sufficiently to force recentralization.

In the face of uncertainty, planning ideally should provide a variety of types of sites. Few communities can provide a complete range, but to the extent possible, this should be a planning goal. This approach also conforms to the experience of most economic developers in that firms generally approach communities with fairly definite notions of the type of site, location, and structure desired. Given the competition between communities, the situation is very much of a buyer's market from the development agency's viewpoint. Firms in manufacturing and distribution are far more likely to change their selection of community, if the desired type of site or structure is not available, than to change their choice of site and structure type. Thus, entirely apart from the matter of uncertainty about the future, being able to offer a wide variety of sites and structures is advantageous in the present.

Within the planning profession, there has been much interest in preservation in recent years. Some of this relates to the saving of buildings with historic or architectural merit. Similarly, there has been much interest in the rehabilitation of existing residential buildings to minimize cost and neighborhood disruption. There is also, in urban areas, a less-often-stated case for preservation of older industrial structures. The old industrial building which is fully depreciated, and which carries low property taxes (as a function of its low market value), can provide a home for firms which cannot afford more expensive quarters.[13] Given the possibility that energy-price increases will force some recentalization, it would appear that preservation of at least some of the stock of older industrial buildings is well advised.

How much public action will be required to move ahead from the planning considerations discussed earlier will vary tremendously. In some instances, land-use control policies alone may be sufficient. More often, use of the community's capital budget to make investments in roads, utility lines, waste-disposal capacity and other infrastructure will also be required. Often, judicious use of land-use controls and off-site investment will still not be sufficient to guarantee adequate developable space, and public-land assemblage, through condemnation or purchase, will also be needed. Where readily developable land is not available for reasons of topography, drainage, or subsoil conditions, public expenditure to render it developable at a competitive price may be needed. Typically, the development agency may acquire property, spend money on grading, piling, drainage, access, demolition, clearance, and other improvements, and then sell or lease the resulting buildable sites at below cost. In some instances, the agency may go still further and construct facilities for lease. However it is done, the common element is the expenditure of public funds to fill the gap between the cost of a buildable site and the market value of that site. In some instances, the funds may come from local sources, public or private. In other instances, as discussed in Chapter 10, there may be a substantial federal contribution.

On occasion, land development is made economically possible by public investment, which changes the demand for land. For example, public investment in convention centers is generally made in the expectation that increasing the demand for commercial location will promote desirable development. In fact, few such facilities are now built without substantial public participation. The presumption is that the public contribution is justified by both the public and private gains resulting from the development attracted by the convention center. Similarly, a certain amount of public subsidy has gone into hotel and motel development on the grounds that lodging facilities are a prerequisite for other types of activity the community wishes to attract.

NOTES

1. At 1980 construction costs, the median cost for parking structures is slightly below $15 per square foot. R.S. Means Co., *Means System Data*, Duxbury, Mass.

2. Maximum flow rates are achieved at about 35 mph. Above that speed flow is lessened because vehicle spacing increases faster than vehicle speed. Below that speed, the reverse is true.

3. The conventional view is that energy shortages (or prices) will increase for the rest of the century. But there are dissenting views. Herman Kahn, of the Hudson Institute, takes the position that the main U.S. energy problem is that of choosing among a number of alternative paths and then making the requisite investment (Hudson Institute Seminar, October 1979). A study by Richard H. Schackson and J. James Leach, for the Energy Productivity Center of the Mellon Institute (1980), projected that the combination of conservation and a moderate rate of synthetic-petroleum consumption would be sufficient to permit American automotive-use patterns to remain essentially unchanged for the remainder of the century. New York *Times*, August 19, 1980, D1.

4. Figures are from 1975, cited in *Statistical Abstract of the United States*, Bureau of the Census, Dept. of Commerce, 1979. Recent data suggest the figure has risen somewhat since that time. A few of the largest metropolitan areas weight this figure very heavily. For example, if the New York metropolitan area figures are subtracted from national totals, the figure falls to close to 4 percent.

5. F. Stuart Chapin and Edward J. Kaiser, *Urban Land Use Planning*, 3rd. ed., University of Illinois Press, Urbana, 1979.

6. Many older zoning ordinances are written in a pyramidal form. The highest use is permitted in any zone and each succeeding use is permitted in the first zone which allows it, plus every lower zone. Thus, if the highest-use zone, as is common, is single-family housing, that use is permitted everywhere. If the second highest use zone is apartments, that use is permitted everywhere except in single-family zones. If the lowest-use zone is heavy industry, that use is permitted only in the heavy-industry zone. The illustration is somewhat simplified in that each of the uses cited above is likely to be broken down into a number of subcategories. Since residential uses are considered higher uses, such an ordinance protects designated residential areas from commercial intrusion but does not protect commercial areas from residential intrusion.

7. R.S. Means Co., op. cit.

8. The suboptimality of zoning for the reasons implied here has been the subject of some academic inquiry. William A. Fischel, "The Property Rights Approach to Zoning," *Land Economics*, February 1978, provides a theoretical discussion of this point.

9. While these numbers are arbitrary, they are not unrealistic for corporate-headquarters development. A number of headquarters in the Westchester/Fairfield County portion of the New York region, including, for example, Pepsico and IBM, approximate such employee-per-acre ratios.

10. Quoted in Donald C. Lochmoeller et al., *Industrial Development Handbook*, Urban Land Institute, Washington, D.C., 1975.

11. Ibid.

12. Although the idea that higher energy costs (or energy shortages, if sufficiently severe) will force recentralization and favor existing urban centers is commonly accepted, it is only a hypothesis at this point. It is conceivable that it will favor a multimodal pattern featuring a high degree of local self-sufficiency—cogeneration for energy conservation, workers' housing close to plants, neighborhood shopping rather than shopping centers.

13. The cost of space varies with time and location, but, as an example of the differential, new manufacturing space in industrial parks in the New York suburbs might rent in the $4-per-square-foot-per-year range while old space in more centrally located multistory structures can be had for $1. The ability of older urban areas to offer small, young, struggling firms low-cost space has been one factor in the ability of urban areas to play an incubator role in the development of new industries and new technologies.

8

PUBLIC RELATIONS, ADVERTISING, AND PROMOTION

Although the subject of this chapter occupies only a small percentage of the space in this book, the activities it describes occupy more of most economic developers' time than any other single activity. In fact, for many practitioners, they occupy most of their time. This is so for several reasons:

• The competition for industry is intense.
• In many cases the advantages of one place over another are relatively minor.
• The cost of gathering information to the firm is high. And, as a result, all decisions are made under conditions of partial ignorance.
• Regardless of how much information a firm may gather and how much thought its officers may apply to the question of location, impressions and intuitions will play some part in the final decision.

It is the combination of intense competition and market imperfection which creates the need for salesmanship, in the most general sense of that word. Were all locational decisions made under conditions of perfect information and complete rationality, there would be no need for this chapter.

For the economic developer, public relations, advertising, and promotion accomplish several goals. First, they initiate communication with firms. Once communication has begun, matters of substance can be explored and communications can become progressively more technical. Second, such activities create interest in the area, which may lead to moves in even if there is no further direct contact between firm and development agency. Finally, promotional and public-relations efforts build political support. Not only does this increase the life expectancy of the agency, but it makes it far more effective. Where there is conflict over economic development or where goals cannot be accomplished without public expenditures, this political support is crucial.

PUBLIC RELATIONS

By public relations is meant all those activities, other than paid advertising, that increase agency visibility, both within and outside the community.

For a large area, such as a state or a very large city, a public-relations campaign designed to change its image may be justified. For a smaller place, such as this book is written for, such an expenditure is rarely justified. The following discusses public-relations that have two main goals: bringing firms into contact with the agency and building political support within the community.

Public relations differs from advertising in that there is no payment for space or time; one does not purchase space in newspapers or magazines, nor time on radio or TV. The products of public-relations efforts come to the reader or listener or viewer as news or as information, not as clearly labeled selling messages. When one sees an ad or hears a commercial, there is no doubt that one is receiving a selling message. One does not generally have that reaction when reading an article in a newspaper. When one reads the business pages, one is reading business news. The sophisticated reader may know that most business news is not ferreted out through diligent reportage, but rather, first comes to the editor's attention through a phone call or press release from the company or from its public-relations counsel. But this fact is not likely to be foremost in the reader's consciousness, no matter how well he may know it intellectually. Public-relations material is thus likely to be much less heavily discounted than advertising. But the other side of this coin is that the advertiser has total control over the message, whereas the sender of a press release can only mail it and hope. The editor to whom it is sent may discard it, use it as sent, or modify it in any way he sees fit. He may call back for more information or he may not. The message may get through as intended or it may be quite distorted. In almost no case, however, will the writer of the release be allowed to see in advance what will appear in print. In fact, to request such a privilege is either to impugn the integrity of the editor or to demonstrate one's own lack of sophistication about such matters.

For public-relations material to see the light of day, an editor must decide that it has some news value. The actions of local government and of economic development agencies do, indeed, constitute news. But their news value falls off rapidly with distance. For most development agencies, then, public-relations activity will largely be restricted to the community and perhaps the immediate surrounding area.

Some agencies will mount their own public-relations effort. Others will use a public-relations counsel. Still other agencies may use a public-relations counsel to develop a campaign and then, when sufficient in-house skill has been developed, will themselves take over the public-relations function. This chapter is written from the perspective of the organization which handles the process itself.

There are two main targets for the public-relations efforts of the development agency. One is the general public. They are to be reached largely for the purpose of building public support for the development program. The second target is the business community. The fact that most businessmen reached will be local should not be a cause for distress. For, as noted earlier, most growth in most areas is internally generated. In the long run, more agency successes are likely to originate locally rather than at a distance. This is particularly true in older urban areas where the real task of the development agency is to prevent further attrition of the local economy.

Three main channels for reaching both groups should be considered: newspapers, the business press, and groups and meetings.

A certain amount of exposure may be gotten through radio, but in the writer's experience, it is a weaker medium for this purpose. Much broadcasting is done during the day, when the number of businessmen listening is low. Then, too, what appears in print can always be torn out for reference later. A message on a talk show caught while one is driving is a good deal more perishable than a newspaper article. Local TV may be used occasionally by some agencies, but it is probably the most difficult medium on which to get exposure.

For newspapers, the primary instrument is the press release. The text of one sent by the agency once headed by the writer is shown below. It obviously did not take a great deal of time to write. Yet it resulted in articles in the New York *Times* and a number of local papers. Purchase of comparable amount of advertising space would have cost some thousands of collars and, for reasons noted earlier, would have been substantially less useful to the agency.

For Information Contact: FOR IMMEDIATE RELEASE
Norman J. Shaw
(914) 682-2499
$1 MILLION WCIDA FINANCING BRINGS BELGIAN FIRM TO WESTCHESTER

As a result of a joint effort of the Westchester County Industrial Development Agency (WCIDA) and the New York State Department of Commerce, WCIDA's second financing, a $1 million bond issue, has been completed. This will enable Ordibel, Inc., the American division of a Belgian company, to expand its U.S. operations to a 40,000 square foot building in Westchester. Aided by tax-exempt financing provided through the WCIDA, Ordibel, a manufacturer of collators and sorters, is moving into a headquarters building at 543 Tarrytown Road, Greenburgh. Ordibel was brought to the WCIDA by William S. Junor, ombudsman of the New York State Department of Commerce.

"We're quite excited that Ordibel will be locating in Westchester," commented County Executive Alfred B. DelBello, "and we are additionally pleased to see continuing cooperation among the various government agencies in the field of economic development. The Ordibel facility in Greenburgh will mean about 100 new jobs for the county, most of them blue-collar. The move of Ordibel, a Belgian company, is particularly gratifying since it demonstrates once again the desirability of Westchester as the location for international corporations."

The bond-purchase arrangements added to the international flavor. Approximately half the bonds were bought by the National Bank of Westchester. The balance of the bonds were purchased by a group of private investors, both foreign and American, and guaranteed by Societe du Belgique, a Belgian bank. The $1 million of bonds were issued for a 10-year term at a rate of 7.25%, resulting in considerable debt service savings for the company.

Anthony C. Clarkson, president of Ordibel, said that the purchase of the Greenburgh building was greatly enhanced by attractive WCIDA financing. He also remarked, "Ordibel was able to secure just the right building for our American headquarters, a building which permits us to establish fabricating and assembling functions as well as general offices. Locating in Westchester allows us to remain close to our most vital commercial and market areas." Mr. Clarkson said that Ordibel had investigated other sites in Illinois, Georgia, New Jersey, and Connecticut before choosing Westchester.

Press releases are usually written in the so-called inverted-pyramid style, as are most news articles. That is, they can be cut from the bottom without the sense of the story being lost. As a rule of thumb, the questions of who, what, where, when, and why ought to be covered in the first sentence. For example:

James Smith, director of the East Nowhere Economic Development Agency, will address the East Nowhere Rotary Club on "Financing New Industry" this Thursday at noon at Alfredo's Steak House. The agency, founded last April, is now beginning a program to . . . .

If only the first sentence is printed by a paper, the reader is at least informed that a development agency exists, that its head is James Smith, and that it has something to do with financing new industry.

The release should be printed on letterhead which identifies the issuing agency. It may have a release date or it may say "for immediate release." Which to use depends on which and how many papers are sent the release. Most editors will not use a piece if it has appeared previously in a competing paper. To prevent an editor from not using the release because he has been scooped, a release date may be advisable. Most editors will respect the date and not use the story before that date.

Next, the release should have a headline. This is a convenience for the editor in that it tells him quickly what the story is about. There should be a name and phone number placed before or after the text, so that an editor or reporter can call for more details.

What constitutes a publicizable event? Obviously, any agency accomplishment is publicizable. But since the agency will be in existence for many months or perhaps even several years before there are concrete accomplishments, almost anything the agency or its personnel do should be considered publicizable. For example, the creation of the agency and the appointment of personnel or board members are newsworthy. When the agency produces data items, such as lists of available sites, maps, brochures, their availability is publicizable. As discussed subsequently, a certain amount of public speaking and of meeting with groups is useful. Each time an agency member goes out to address a Rotary club or Lion's club or county bar-association meeting, it is a publicizable event.

How much publicity an agency should seek is a matter for individual judgment. The agency should seek to make its existence and role well known to the public and the business community. Though visibility is desirable, inflated claims should be avoided and false expectations should not be created. Financings and other arrangements in process should not be publicized until they become 100 percent certainties. Short-term visibility should not be gained at the price of long-term credibility.

Beyond the press release, there may be opportunities for increasing agency visibility through writing for the local press. How many there are depends on the area. If there is a local business press, it should be an early target. One way to approach the business press is by writing a brief letter to the editor describing a proposed article and the writer and inquiring as to whether the article is of interest. A letter to the editor of a newsletter addressed to real estate brokers might begin as follows:

> In a highly competetive industrial real estate market, the broker's ability to put together an attractive financial package may be the difference between making and losing a sale. Tax-exempt financing can provide the capital for acquisition, construction, or renovation of industrial space at several percentage points below the prime rate. Our agency is empowered to issue such financing for qualified companies. Do you think your readers would be interested in an article . . . ?

A letter to the editor of a local weekly business newspaper might begin:

> The county has recently established an office of economic development to promote commercial and industrial growth. Among its functions will be the dissemination of information, smoothing the

relationships between government and business, and providing development financing to qualified firms. Would your readers be interested in an article which ... ?

The local business press is generally not difficult to get into. Many local business papers are essentially scissor-and-pase operations in that they rely primarily on press releases and contributed pieces rather than on staff-written articles; the number of readers reached is not large, but they are the audience that the development agency needs most to reach.

Local newspapers can also be approached in the same general manner as suggested above (a brief letter identifying the author and suggesting the subject of the article).

As an alternative to, or in addition to, the placed article, one should also consider the invited interview. For example, one might call the editor of the business page of the local newspaper and inquire as to whether he or she would be interested in doing a piece on the agency—why it was set up, what it does, how it sees the local economy, who is on its staff.

Another source of exposure to the business community, and to the body politic more generally, is public speaking. The Rotary, Lions, Kiwanis, and other groups that meet periodically need speakers on a regular basis. A letter to the program chairman of the Rotary, for example, may get one a considerable number of speaking engagements over the course of the year. Basically, the same talk—on why the agency exists, how it sees the local situation, what it does—can be used repeatedly. Speaking makes the agency known in the business community and also gives agency personnel another window on what is happening in the area. Before-and-after speech conversations, and even questions asked at the end of the speech, are useful toward this end. Beyond such general-purpose business groups as the Rotary, there are specialized groups which can be reached. Among these are associations of accounts, lawyers, bankers, and real estate brokers. These are all categories of people who have a network of connections within the business community. In speaking to such groups, the talk should be tailored to group interests. One might speak to bankers about tax-exempt financing, and to realtors about how the development agency and commercial realtors might cooperate. Speaking to nonbusiness groups is not likely to have the same effect of generating inquiries and making contacts, but it may have other uses. For example, speaking to the League of of Women Voters might be useful in building a political base. Again, the talk should be adjusted to the audience. League members might be rather bored by development financing, but quite interested in a discussion of local and regional economic trends, or of the future of the municipal tax base. A local conservation group might be addressed on the subject of balancing economic needs and environmental goals. Labor unions should also be on the list of potential audiences, partly for reasons of building a base of poltical support and partly for contacts with firms.

In addition to the above, there are some classes of people with whom it is well to meet on a private or small-group basis. Virtually every business move or expansion will involve a commercial banker at some stage. It is therefore extremely useful for bankers to know of the agency and what it does. The most direct route is to call, explain what you are about, and set up a lunch or other meeting date. Commercial real estate brokers are another group with whom rapport is essential. They can be approached in the same way. Brokers are an invaluable source of information and contacts.

As the work of the agency proceeds, there will be considerable interaction with brokers. Firms which have become interested in the area will want referrals to brokers. The agency may obtain information on buildings and sites from brokers. Brokers may use agency literature and studies as selling tools. If the agency has financing capabilities, brokers may bring potential customers to the agency to discuss the all-important question of money. There is, generally, a community of interests between the development agency and the commercial real estate brokerage community

With regard to the real estate community, there is, however, a point of potential conflict or friction and it is well to discuss it in advance. In one sense, the operations of a development agency are a boon to the commercial real estate industry. Increased interest in the area brings in potential customers, and this implies the possibility of increased sales (and commissions). On the other hand, if a firm learns of a building or parcel of land through a development agency and goes directly to the owner, a broker may lose a commission. In addition, there is the question of how development agencies will refer firms to brokers.

To avoid hard feelings and possible litigation, it is well for the agency and the local real estate community to come to an agreement on how this will be handled. One technique is to put together a list of commercial brokers and give the list to inquirers without commenting on the relative merits of each firm. Another method might be to simultaneously mail the firm's name and interests to every broker on a list, with the understanding that it is then the broker's responsibility to contact the firm. Regardless of how the problem is handled, it should be addressed and solved in advance.

Another goal of such meetings may be the assembling of a common list of available sites. This has the advantage of making information about the area much more accessible, which, from an agency viewpoint, is highly desirable. The intensely competitive nature of the real estate brokerage business, however, may make brokers reluctant to share information sufficiently to create such a list. "All we have to sell is information," as one broker told the author when the idea was first proposed. However, compromise solutions can often be worked out.

Another group with whom it is worth talking early on are commercial builders. Most agencies have a financing function, and this is a central consideration when a builder and a firm set down to talk. Therefore, it is well for the builder to be aware of the agency and its capabilities.

ADVERTISING

Because the actions of the development agency generally cease to be news once the area boundary is crossed, paid advertising may be necessary to reach a nonlocal audience.

Unlike consumer advertising which may, by itself, sell the product, area advertising only initiates communication. Therefore, it should not be begun until the agency is able to follow it up adequately. For example, in response to an inquiry generated by an ad, a package of information about the area is sent. Then, to begin communication, a representative of the agency calls and inquires as to whether the information has been received. For this to work successfully, the agency's entire operation should be in a state of readiness. Brochures, data sheets, maps, should be on hand. If additional information is needed, it should be available; any service the literature boasts of should be in a state of readiness. If the initial material sent out indicates that the agency has the capacity to arrange tax-exempt financing, the entity which issues such financing should be in existence and ready to function. If the agency has decided that part of its followup will consist of having area businessmen communicate their experiences to potential new firms, then a network of contacts should have already been made. In short, the followup system should make the agency appear competent and professional. Advertising with little followup behind it creates expectations which can't be fulfilled and causes the agency to lose credibility. It may have some short-run political payoff for the agency, by giving the impression that the agency is doing something, but in the long run it is not productive.

What media should be considered? In most cases, area advertising means magazine advertising. In some cases, the business sections or the business supplements of newspapers may be used. Radio advertising, from what the writer has observed, is relatively ineffective.

For magazine advertising, there are a limited number of magazines for use that are specifically devoted to economic development and location. Among these are *Area Development, American Industrial Properties Report, Northeast Industrial Reporter, Plant Sites and Parks.* These publications are generally controlled circulation magazines—qualified readers receive them without cost. Readership is confined to people who are of interest to advertisers, and the publication's sole source of income is advertising revenue. One such publication lists the categories of readers as "Chairmen, Presidents, owners, chief executive officers, vice presidents, treasurers, real estate managers and corporate managers." Circulation figures are audited, and the reader must periodically indicate his desire to continue receiving the publication. The publication noted above, one of the larger ones in the field, quotes circulation of about 32,000. Thus, the circulations of such publications do not compare with consumer magazines or major newspapers. On the other hand, their content and their readership are appropriate to the interests of a development agency. Advertising rates vary from one publication to another but, in general, are under $2,000 a page. A one-third-page ad might thus cost $600 to $800 per issue, depending upon the publication, number of times run per year, etc. For the type of publication mentioned above, ad cost per reader would be somewhat under three cents.

For an advertising budget of, say, $10,000 per year. it is possible to run perhaps a dozen ads. For the beginning agency, one approach is to try several publications to get an idea of the number and quality of inquiries that each provides. If an ad is run frequently in the same publication, there will tend to be fewer inquiries per ad than if it is run occasionally, though the total number of inquiries will be greater. Therefore, even though on a one-time basis, one publication may prove superior on a cost-per-serious-inquiry basis, there is still a case to be made for distributing an advertising budget among several publications. In terms of followup, it is wise to spread the advertising over the year. This enables the agency to provide thorough followup. If advertising is bunched in one part of the year, a certain amount of followup will be delayed or done hastily, and this does not make a good first impression.

Advertising in more general business publications can be considered but may not be practical for a small agency. For example, a full page in *Business Week* costs, at this writing, over $17,000, and about two cents per reader. Unless the agency has a very large budget for advertising, one or two half-page or one-third page ads may exhaust it.

General-circulation magazines offer somewhat lower per-reader costs but absolute rates can run very high. For example, *Time* magazine costs about one cent per reader for a full-page ad, but the ad costs about $45,000. The more general the audience of the magazine, the smaller will be the percentage of the audience of interest to the agency. For the above reasons, the use of specialized publications such as those noted earlier is usually the best way for a new agency to begin. A certain amount of experimentation is also advisable.

Newspaper advertising in commerce and industry supplements or in business sections produces a larger number of inquiries per dollar spent than do ads in specialized publications. But in the writer's experience, the inquiries tend to be of much lower quality.

Most area advertising is not particularly creative, as is some consumer advertising. The basic format is to state a few area advantages (favorable labor markets, central location, lower-cost power, available sites, quality of life) and provide the name and address of a person the reader can contact. Most of the specialized publications, like most trade magazines, provide a reader-inquiry or reader-service card so that, by checking off numbers on a single card, the reader can receive literature from as many advertisers as desired. The general style in area advertising can readily be checked by reference to a few of the publications mentioned earlier.

Public relations and advertising are largely generators of inquiries. Most development agencies also contact firms directly. For a small agency, time available for cold calls may be limited. A reasonable amount of effort in public relations and advertising is likely to generate sufficient activity to leave little time for direct contact. As staff grows, man-hours for direct contact become available. Approaches to direct contact vary widely.

One place to begin is in one's own area. It may sound odd to advise starting with firms already there, but there is a certain logic to it. As stated before, the major share of growth in most areas is internally generated. If this is so, then a major part of what one might call outreach effort should be devoted to local industry. One goal is retention. If one communicates with firms, one has a chance to deal with problems before they cause firms to move out. Very often, firms are unaware of what can be done for them. It cannot be overemphasized that the workings of government often appear quite opaque to firms. This is particularly so of smaller firms where all personnel have operating responsibilities and there are no purely staff people who have time to research questions. At one time, the writer had dealings with a small jobber in aircraft parts. The firm distributed various fittings, fasteners, seals. It generally received a truckload of parts per day and shipped them out in small packages by parcel post. In terms of impact on the community, it was little different from a small office. The firm owned land and wanted to expand on it. Unfortunately, the zoning law specified that no more than 25 percent of floor space might be warehousing. The firm, needing to store a large inventory, required a facility which was 75 percent storage and 25 percent offices—the reverse of what the zoning permitted. The firm's needs, though they clearly violated the letter of the law, did not violate the intent of the law. But, because of the problem, the firm was on the verge of moving. The author's agency counseled the firm on how to present its case to the zoning board and then wrote a rough draft of an appeal from the firm to the board. Without too much delay, a zoning variance was obtained. On another occasion, the owner of a small manufacturing firm indicated to the writer that he intended to move his operation out of New York State and into the adjacent state of Connecticut. On inquiry, it turned out that the firm was expanding and had to move from its present quarters. The reason for moving to Connecticut was that Connecticut offered tax-exempt financing through the Connecticut Development Authority (CDA). After the owner described the financing package offered, the writer asked whether he was aware that essentially the same package was available in New York State. The answer was no and the move was forestalled. Had the contact not occurred until after the owner signed a contract on property in Connecticut, the firm would have moved. Early contacts with companies are thus essential.

To bring about such contact, the development agency must often make the first move. A coworker of the writer's approached the matter in a very simple and quite successful way. After the agency had decided that manufacturing production was the weakest segment of the area's economy, he obtained a list of some 200 manufacturing firms. He then wrote a letter to each, which began, "How can we help you? We are . . . ," and which then went on briefly to state the agency's function, ending with a statement that he would call shortly to set up an interview. The response was very positive, and several businessmen indicated that this was the first time anyone from the government had called them with the intention of doing something for them rather than to them.

Once sufficient contact with firms inside the area has been made, the question of outside contact arises. The techniques for doing this vary enormously. Some are described below.

Selecting a Target List

One place to begin is by selecting a target list of industries. Having reviewed the area's relative strengths and weaknesses, as suggested in Chapter 6, an industry-by-industry evaluation can be made. A systematic listing of all industries can be found in the *Standard Industrial Classification Manual* (SIC manual).[1]

One technique is to go through the manual and consider activities, industrial or otherwise, whose needs appear to match area characteristics. A small number of relatively promising ones can be picked out. Further research, consisting, at least in part, of interviews with firms now in the field, will strengthen or negate the researcher's initial impression.

When a target group has been selected, a list of firms in the field can be developed from industry directories. A phone call or a phone call preceded by a letter can be used to initiate communication. One development consultant has made successful use of intermediaries in this regard. For example, assume that an area in question has a good supply of engineering and skilled manufacturing workers and low power costs. The economic developer concludes that injection molding is an activity which could prosper in this area. The developer might then ask a local injection molder to provide introductions to his colleagues in other areas, or perhaps to allow the developer to write a letter, for the molder's signature, addressed to some of his colleagues. As a variation, one might enlist the aid of a local buyer of injection moldings to help contact some of his suppliers in the same way.

In a more general sense, any network of contacts the economic developer can establish is likely to be useful. For example, a development agency might set up a businessmen's advisory council whose members use their own business connections both to learn of impending moves and expansions and to interest nonlocal firms (customers, suppliers) in the area. As pointed out earlier, businessmen generally favor growth even when their own interests are not visibly served by growth, so that setting up such a council should not be unduly difficult.

To whatever extent possible, the participation of the business community should be sought. Businessmen bring an expertise in a particular field that is virtually impossible for someone from the outside to match, and their presence is reassurance of the existence of a harmonious government/business relationship. Where government is, in effect, in partnership with a developer, it is often well to let the developer take the lead in contacting prospective firms, with agency personnel serving to represent government interests, respond to technical questions about the role of government in the development, and provide assurance that public participation will be constructive and effective.

Another way that particular industries can be approached is through trade shows. Though they are an excellent way to make contacts, expenses for creating a display, for travel and lodging, and space rental can be high. Thus, participation must be selective.

Finally, a number of development agencies will simply have their personnel make direct calls on firms which they regard as possible inmigrants. Like any other salesman, the development agency representative walks in and makes the case for his product—in this case a particular city or state or county.

In some cases, agencies will maintain offices in areas from which they believe firms can be pried loose. A number of southern states maintain offices in New York City. Their function is to approach firms with the intention of interesting them in relocation. The combination of a large number of firms, high local taxes, high costs of doing business, and a variety of urban problems makes the city a good source of firms that might be approached. Whether one should regard this type of activity as a legitimate form of competition or as essentially destructive is arguable. There seems little doubt that it is reasonably successful.[2]

THE DEVELOPMENT DATA BASE

There is not much point in mounting an extensive public-relations and advertising effort if the questions that effort produces cannot be answered. Given the difficulty of developing area information, the agency which can offer a comprehensive information package about its area has a substantial advantage over the agency which cannot. Developing a data base for a large county, for example, takes a considerable amount of time. In the writer's experience, even for an area about which much information has been developed for planning, promotional, and other purposes, the task of putting together a good development data base can easily absorb a man-year or more. For an area in which little groundwork has been done for other purposes, considerably more effort may be required. In the long run, however, the effort is well worthwhile. Some elements of the data base are listed below:

● Maps. The following information should be mapped:
 political boundaries
 location with respect to other areas
 major transportation routes
 secondary road patterns
 areas served by public water and sewers
 areas served by gas and electricity (unless the entire area is so served); if different utilities serve different areas, their service areas should be indicated.
 zoning and land use.
 topography and major environmental features
 demographic data, including population density, personal income, recent rate of population growth, value of housing (of particular interest to retailers)
 traffic volume of major routes
 maps showing major concentrations of economic activity (of interest to firms who sell their services to other firms)

● To the extent possible, the map series should have common logotypes, possibly a standard size and scale.

● Population data: statistics including numbers of residents, age, sex, race, personal income, occupation, education, recent growth trends.

● Economic data, including employment by major sector, lists of major firms, retail sailes, wage rates by occupational category, unemployment rates.

● Taxes: types of taxes and rates (sales, income, business taxes). For property taxes, average burden per $1,000 of full value is a useful statistic.

● Utilities: rates and names of suppliers. Where the structure of rates is complex, as with electricity, an average per-unit cost for industrial and commercial suppliers, rather than the complete pattern, should be shown.

● The structure of government: a brief picture of the structure of government. Information on the regulatory activities of government including land-use controls, environmental reviews, discharge permits. The emphasis should not be on comprehensive description but on who does what and who one contacts to find out the details.

● Financing assistance: a list of programs that may be organized, either by type of program or by agency or level of government responsible for the program.

● Amenities: a list of major cultural, educational, and recreational facilities should be included. This does not mean listing every vest-pocket park and elementary school, but rather major and/or distinctive institutions and facilities.

● Site information: if possible, a list of sites suitable for development should be prepared. The following data for each site are suggested:
 shape, size, and topography
 proximity to sewer, water, electric, and gas lines
 proximity to nearest main road (also, rail access if nearby)

assessed value of site (with conversion to full value if the area does not use full-value assessment)

estimated property tax burdern per $1,000 of full value of development

zoning

ownership

In developing the data base, it is easy to err on the side of deluging the inquirer with every possible item and many localities do this. A nonintimidating basic information package should be worked up, and very detailed materials left on the agency shelf to be used when the particular occasion arises. The data should be put into a data book, or a brief series of brochures, rather than into a mass of loose sheets. A printed jacket with inside pockets for brochures and data sheets is a common and effective persentation form. It has the advantage that the contents can be varied for different firms.

The list above is not absolutely complete. Different localities have different characteristics and presumably should offer somewhat different sets of information.

NOTES

1. *Standard Industrial Classification Manual,* Bureau of the Budget, Government Printing Office, Washington, D.C. This book provides a systematic listing of all major types of economic activity, under about 95 two-digit headings. These, in turn, are broken up into three- and four-digit headings. For example, category 36 is electric machinery and supplies. Under this heading is 361, which is electric transmission and distribution equipment; a subgroup of that is 3,611, which is electric measurement instruments and test equipment. Of the 95 or so two-digit headings, manufacturing constitutes 21 headings. Transportation, communications, and utilities take up several other two-digit headings; wholesaling and retailing, another several headings; finance, insurance, and real estate, another several headings, and so on.

2. Most economic development activity is suffused with the fundamental problem that one area's gain is another area's loss. In the writer's experience, most economic developers confine their loyalty to the jurisdiction which pays their salary and do not worry about the question. For the philosophically inclined, an argument can be constructed that the net result of economic development activity in the United States is the dissemination of information and a more efficient pattern of industrial and commercial location. The giving of subsidies, direct and indirect, might be considered to have aggregate effects analogous to a general reduction in the cost of capital, with, presumably, the effect of increasing total investment. One can argue, to the contrary, that that is largely a zero sum game. One might go further and say that the assiduous wooing of industry, to the extent that it further pulls apart shaky urban economies, is a destructive activity which runs counter to national urban policy.

9

OVERVIEW OF
FINANCIAL ASSISTANCE PROGRAMS

Since financial assistance programs are what might be termed "unconventional" financing, a familiarity with conventional real estate financing is useful. However, no chapter on conventional financing is provided in this book since the subject is covered in many texts on real estate. For the convenience of the reader, a few concepts related to real estate financing are briefly discussed in Appendix B.

A wide variety of financial incentives is offered to industry in an effort to promote local economic development. As noted earlier, there seems to be little doubt among those who have studied it that subsidization is more influential at the intraregional rather than the interregional level. Because so many communities offer comparable types of assistance, it might be that the total pattern of industrial development in the United States would not be radically different than it is were no communities to offer any sort of assistance. Nonetheless, the community which failed to offer any types of assistance would be at a significant disadvantage.

The development agency is generally interested in getting firms to make a long-term commitment to the community, whether this be the decision of a local firm to renovate or expand its facility, or the decision of an out-of-town firm to move in. For this reason, much more effort has generally been put into programs which encourage investment than into programs which involve operating assistance and short-term finance.[1]

TYPES OF ASSISTANCE

The following material briefly categorizes types of development assistance. The following chapter will describe some federal programs in detail. There is so much variation in state and local programs that no attempt will be made to describe them systematically.

Tax Abatement

At the local level, tax abatement usually takes the form of reduced property taxes. Obviously, the approaches vary widely. Generally, abatement is time limited. There may be complete abatement for a period of years, partial abatement for a period of years, or abatement along a sliding scale. As an example of the latter, New York State has a local-option abatement program in which new commercial construction receives a 50 percent abatement the first year, a 45 percent abatement the second year, and so on until the abatement ends entirely with the tenth year.[2] In areas in which property taxes are rising rapidly, a tax-stabilization arrangement may be used. In this case, the firm receives no abatement but merely a guarantee that taxes will not rise (or not rise more than a stated amount) for a designated time period.

In general, those who have studied the effect of subsidization on industrial location have not found property-tax abatement a major inducement to industral location. One difficulty in the use of such subsidization is that it is difficult to avoid giving the abatement to some firms which would have located in the area in any case. For example, the New York State program described above requires that the abatement be given either to all eligible firms or to none. The municipality does not have the legal power to differentiate among firms.

From the municipal viewpoint, another aspect of real property-tax abatement to be considered is that the entire cost is borne by the municipality itself (except to the very limited extent that reduced local revenue capacity may result in increased aid from higher levels of government). This is in contrast to most types of financing provided by development agencies, as will become evident.

A small property-tax abatement for new industry, particularly of a limited duration, may cost the community relatively little, yet provide a strong indication of a favorable business climate. Of itself, it may be insufficient to affect firm behavior, yet it may be valuable as part of a total effort to present a favorable image.

In addition to the formal reduction of real estate taxes under various state or local programs, there is also undoubtedly a certain amount of informal reduction that simply takes the form of an unwritten agreement between firm and municipality to underassess. Thus, a sub-rosa approach may actually be more effective from the community viewpoint because it is selective. On the other side of the coin, it holds obvious potential for corruption.

Perhaps more inportant than property-tax abatements is an even-handed pattern of assessment.[3] A pattern in which commercial property is assessed at a higher percentage of market value than residential property is quite common. Politically, it is often very popular because homeowners far outnumber commercial-property owners. It also may be ideologically appealing because it appears to favor the "little guy" against the "big guy." In an immediate sense, the burden of taxation falls only on the property owner because property is immobile and he cannot shift the tax to someone else. If he pays the tax himself, then it is simply a subtraction from his net income.[4] If he leases on a net basis under which the tenant pays the tax, then higher taxes are ultimately capitalized in a lower net value for the structure or in a lower market rental resulting in a loss of income for the owner. However, in a broader view, a pattern of property taxation that falls to an excessive degree upon commercial property retards the growth of the tax base and decreases employment, thus imposing burdens on other people besides commercial-property owners.

A number of states provide various types of corporate tax abatement. In general, programs abate the taxes of firms which either move into the state or expand within the state. How cost effective such programs are is not known. It is in the interest of the state to grant such abatement only when the abatement will make a difference in the firm's decision. It is in the interest of the firm to make it appear that the abatement is crucial. As a matter of operating reality, the development agency wooing a firm is likely to offer the firm everything it can. Thus, the role of any one incentive is even less clear than the role of the complete incentive package.

Investment Credits. Investment credits are another commonly offered incentive at the state level. A certain percentage of the firm's investment in the plant and/or capital equipment may be deducted from the firm's state corporate income tax liability. The exemption may be selective or it may be across the board. A selective exemption is likely to be more cost effective than an across-the-board approach, though the latter appears to be more fair and avoids the opportunity for corruption and favoritism.

Loan and Mortgage Guarantees. These are programs which shift the burden of risk from the private lender to the public—usually the state—to make financing available in marginal cases. By a marginal case is meant the instance in which the firm in question appears to have reasonably good prospects for being able to repay but does not have quite strong enough credit to obtain financing strictly on its own merits. If the firm does repay, there is no cost to the state other than the administrative cost of the program. Many of these programs are highly cost effective. They avoid the inevitable question, arising with most forms of subsidization, of whether development would have occurred in any case; and the state incurs expenses, other than administrative costs, in only a small minority of cases. Even these expenses may be avoided by one-time origination charges that include both administrative expenses and a risk premium.

Loan guarantees may also be combined with other types of incentive financing. For example, in some states guarantees are offered for tax-exempt financing. In this form of financing, the real costs are shifted to the federal government (or to the nation as a whole). The guarantee by the state simply enables a larger number of firms within the state to take advantage of an implicit federal subsidy. Again the state may absorb the loss from an occasional bad loan or it may spread this loss to all users of the program by including a risk premium in its front-end charges.

Second-Mortgage Financing. The second-mortgage process resembles loan and mortgage guarantees in that the state or the municipality, by assuming a certain amount of risk, encourages private lenders to make loans in circumstances where they would otherwise be hesitant. The usual arrangement is for the public body to act as the second mortgagee. This reduces the exposure of the bank or other financial institution providing a conventional first mortgage. In addition to helping to make conventional first mortgages available, it also may have the secondary effect of decreasing the amount of the owner's equity required. For example, New York State's Job Development Authority (JDA) provides second mortgages up to 40 percent of project cost. A typical financing plan might be composed of 10 percent owner's equity, 50 percent conventional financing, and 40 percent second mortgage from JDA. The reduction in owner's equity and hence the increase in leverage are quite substantial, for conventional mortgages typically do not cover more than 75 percent of cost.

In many such programs, including the one just mentioned, the second-mortgage money comes from bonds issued by the state or the agency and the bonds are repaid by payments from the mortgagors. The rate at which the agency lends is set sufficiently high to cover the losses from an occasional default. Because the state can borrow in tax-exempt markets, the interest rates can be attractive. As in all tax-exempt financing, most of the cost is shifted to the federal government. Such programs are highly cost effective from the issuing jurisdiction's perspective.

Interest-Rate Reductions. Numerous programs involve reduced-interest loans. Generally, the state or locality picks up part of the interest cost of a financing to reduce debt-service costs and make the project more attractive to the entrepreneur. The cost of the interest-rate reduction is borne by the state or locality as a whole. Cost effectiveness is questionable. If it could be known with certainty that the development would not have occurred in the absence of writedown, revenue/cost or benefit/cost calculations could be made. These calculations, in themselves, involve some degree of uncertainty with regard to such factors as multiplier effect and cost of additional public services. But to this uncertainty is added the problem of determining the probability that the development would not have occurred without subsidization. Thus, to get the benefits for the benefit/cost ratio, one must multiply one uncertainty by another.

Tax-Exempt Financing.　In tax-exempt financing (to be described in detail in the following chapter) a public body finances development by issuing bonds whose interest is tax exempt. In general, interest is exempt from both state and federal taxation, but in some special cases it may be exempt from one and not the other.

Because the interest on the loan constitutes tax-exempt income for the lender, interest costs are substantially reduced. This type of financing thus delivers a subsidy both to borrower and lender. The borrower obtains money at substantially less than conventional interest rates while the lender receives increased after-tax income (even though his before-tax income is lower).

Tax-exempt financing may be coupled with other types of subsidy, such as direct-interest subsidy, and may or may not involve guarantees by state or local government.

For the issuing jurisdiction, it tends to be quite cost effective for one simple reason. Most of the cost is shifted to the federal government because the subsidy primarily consists of the exemption of interest from federal income taxation. As a secondary matter, the administrative costs to the issuing jurisdiction are often rendered nil by the simple device of taking a charge for administrative costs off the top of the issue. In other words, the user of the financing receives a sum which is the net of the agency's administrative costs.

Given the above, even if a substantial number of the projects financed with the tax-exempt bonds would have occurred in any case, the issuing jurisdiction comes out ahead.[5]

Direct Grants and Cost Writedowns.　The variety in this category is enormous. In some cases, assistance may consist of selling or leasing publicly owned property at below cost or below market value. The sale or lease of urban-renewal land, or the long-term lease of land in a municipally owned industrial park would be examples. In some states, municipalities may use their own bonding and taxing powers to build industrial facilities that are then leased to firms at rents which are below debt-service costs. In other cases, development-infrastructure costs may be shared. Much funding from the EDA is of this type. In a number of southern states, state manpower training agencies will pretrain manufacturing-plant work forces, with the major share of training costs being absorbed by the states.

In view of the variety of such programs, both in the nature of the aid offered and the source of the funding, it would be foolish to make categorical statements about the cost effectiveness of this category.

SOME GENERALIZATIONS

Three themes in the preceding may have caught the reader's notice. Let us briefly make them explicit.

• With almost any form of subsidization, there is the question of whether the activity or the project would have occurred in any case. Thus, there is doubt as to whether the subsidy constitutes the crucial inducement or whether it is simply a windfall.

• In many forms of economic development subsidization, there is a separation between those who pay and those who benefit. Where higher levels of government pick up most or all of the bill, the locality is paying with someone else's money. Cost effectiveness is thus, in part, a matter of whose interests are being considered.

• Most, if not all, subsidies distribute benefits to parties other than the explicit beneficiary. An example would be the tax-exempt financing in which benefits accrue to borrower, lender, and municipality, and, ultimately, the labor force. The late Arthur Okun likened the giving of subsidies to carrying water from one place to another in a leaky bucket. Most economic development subsidization programs demonstrate Okun's leaky bucket quite readily.[6]

NOTES

1. In stagnant or declining areas, an economic development agency may be able to do little to bring in new business but much to retain existing business. Under these circumstances, revolving-loan funds, local development corporations, and other entities which can lend working capital may accomplish a great deal. This may be especially true in ghetto areas in which conventional lenders are hesitant to take risks.

2. Program 485-b: The program applies to all new commercial construction with a value of more than $10,000.

3. In many states, the law requires that all classes of properties be assessed on the same basis. Thus, if factories are assessed at 50 percent of market value, so too must single-family houses. Quite often, such laws are widely ignored.

4. It could be argued that where there is a net lease providing for a tax or tax increase falls upon the tenant for the remainder of the lease. When the lease expires, the burden is then shifted to the owner as noted in the text.

5. The attractivness of tax-exempt financing to localities is indicated by the fact that in 1979, industrial-revenue bond issues under $10 million totaled approximately $7 billion. *Wall Street Journal*, October 8, 1980, p. 56.

6. See Arthur Okun, *Equality and Efficiency: The Big Tradeoff*, The Brookings Institute, Washington, D.C., 1975.

10

FEDERAL ASSISTANCE FOR
LOCAL ECONOMIC DEVELOPMENT

This chapter sketches several of the major federal funding programs available to the local economic developer. Program details and funding emphases change frequently, so that this chapter should be regarded simply as a general sketch, to be filled out by making a detailed inquiry at the appropriate federal agency. Because program literature and citations from relevant legislation and passages in the *Federal Register* are readily available from the agencies mentioned in this chapter, program descriptions and regulations are not documented in most cases.

TAX-EXEMPT FINANCING

Tax exempt financing assistance differs from all others to be discussed in this chapter in that it involves a tax expenditure rather than a direct grant. No money flows from the federal government to the firm or locality. Rather, the contribution of the federal government takes the form of tax forgiveness because the federal government, under provisions of the Internal Revenue Service (IRS) code, regards the interest on certain securities as being tax exempt. Another way in which tax-exempt financing differs from direct grants is that the issuing agency, state or local, can commit the federal government to this tax expenditure without prior consultation.

Tax-exempt financing is likely to be the economic developer's single most useful financial tool. It delivers a large subsidy; it can be arranged quickly through an essentially nonbureaucratic, nongovernmental procedure; and it is not competitive. This last point means that there is no fixed pot of money for which projects must compete. There is no ranking or prioritizing of projects. If the proposed project meets the meaning of the appropriate state law and of IRS code provisions, it can be done.

As noted earlier, tax exempt financing may or may not involve guarantees by state or local governments and it may or may not involve other forms of subsidization.

How It Works: A Pure Case

To illustrate the process, let us consider a pure case in which there are no guarantees and no other forms of subsidization. In order to encourage development, a municipality sets up a public-benefit corporation under appropriate provisions of the state law. The agency is empowered to issue tax-exempt financing for industrial and commercial development that serves a public purpose. The public purpose is broadly defined as that of providing jobs and increasing the tax base. The tax-exempt status of bonds stems from provisions of the Internal Revenue code pertaining to what are commonly referred to as "exempt small issues."[1]

The process works in the following manner: A manufacturer approaches the agency and indicates that he would like to build a plant in the community, but that he will not do so without some financial inducement. The agency reviews the firm's application and determines that having the firm in the community would serve the public purpose for which the agency was created, and that the firm indeed will not build the facility without financial inducement. The agency then passes what is commonly referred to as an "inducement resolution," which, in effect, puts the agency in the position of supporting the project.

The firm, having been thus induced to consider locating in the community, now looks for financing. Usually, the first place to look is at the commercial bank with which the firm normally does business. However, other financial institutions or wealthy individuals may also be approached. Since the interest on the securities is tax exempt, the buyer of the bonds will be a party in a high-enough tax bracket to make use of tax-sheltered income. When the terms of financing have been arranged, the firm returns to the agency. If the buyer of the bonds is to be a bank, the terms of the financing are expressed in what is usually termed a "bank commitment letter." This will specify the interest rate, terms, manner of payment, what circumstances constitute default, and may impose various requirements on the firm, such as debt-to-equity ratios. After the firm returns to the agency with its financing arranged, the agency's bond counsel draws up a bond resolution, which permits the agency to issue bonds, in its name, to finance this project. The agency's bond counsel then handles the remaining paperwork connected with the financing.

When the process is completed, the following has been done: Bonds issued by the agency have been bought by a bank (or other lender). The moneys obtained have been deposited in a construction fund. A trustee has been appointed (usually a commercial bank). Acting as an agent for the trustee, the company can draw upon the construction proceeds. When construction is completed, the facility is the property of the development agency. However, the development agency has assigned all rights and responsibilities to the trustee. The company leases the facility from the agency. Its lease payments to the agency cover debt service, payments in lieu of property taxes (a point to be explained shortly), and some miscellaneous items, such as insurance and the trustee's fee.

Although the agency is the owner of record, the IRS recognizes the company as the "beneficial owner" and permits the firm to claim depreciation on the facility. This may appear as a minor point, but is actually quite central. Were firms not allowed to claim this right of ownership, it is dubious that many tax-exempt financings would occur. Just as the firm can claim depreciation on the property as it it owned it, so too does the firm treat the property as its own for accounting purposes. The value of the property appears as an asset on the firm's books and the outstanding debt on the bonds, as a liability.

When the bonds have been retired, the agency then transfers ownership of the plant to the firm. The arrangements for this are specified in the closing papers, signed when the bonds are issued. A common arrangement is for the facility to change hands for $1.

During the period in which the plant is owned by the agency, it is exempt from property taxation because of the agency's status as a public-benefit corporation. However, it is customary for the firm to make payments in lieu of property taxes to the various taxing jurisdictions in which it is located. These payments which are also specified in the closing papers, are routed to the jurisdictions by the trustee.

From the agency's point of view, the transaction is essentially costless. Not only have the bond counsel's fees been paid off the top, but many agencies also charge for their services. If, for example, the agency charges 1 percent of the face amount of the issue (a common charge) and the bond counsel charges $15,000 for services, then for a $1 million bond issue, the company will net $975,000.

The bonds are not an obligation of the agency, but are secured only by a lien on the facility and by whatever other security may have been agreed upon between company and lender. Should the company default on its lease payments, the trustees acting for the bondholders can foreclose. But the bondholders have no claim on any public moneys. These are revenue bonds to be paid off solely by the revenues of the project they finance. They are not, like general-obligation bonds, claims against any level of government.

Because there is no public guarantee behind the issuance of industrial-revenue bonds, only companies with good credit ratings can use them. There have been few if any defaults on such issues, a fact which testifies to this point. Although most issuing agencies will not pass an inducement resolution for a firm whose financial status looks shaky, examination of the firm's financial status is ultimately a responsibility of the bond buyer because it is the bond buyer whose money is at risk.

Because of the front-end costs associated with tax-exempt financing, the technique cannot be used for small issues. As a rule of thumb, an issue of less than $250,000 is not likely to be worth doing. There is, with some exceptions, an upper limit of $10 million.[2] If total project costs exceed $10 million as measured three years backward and three years forward from the date of issue, the tax-exempt status of the bonds is lost. When tax-exempt financings first came into use, there was no upper limit and some of the largest corporations used them for huge projects. Congress determined that this was not the intent of the law and, in the late 1960s amended the IRS code to contain a $5 million capital-spending limit. As of January 1, 1979, the capital-spending limit was raised to $10 million in recognition of the inflation of the preceding decade.

The savings to be had from tax-exempt financing are considerable. A variety of factors, including the state of the market for tax-exempt paper, the creditworthiness of the borrower, and the term of the bonds, affects the differential between conventional and tax-exempt financing. The following financing is one the author helped to set up in the late 1970s when the prime rate was 10 percent: The company was a small, successful manufacturing firm, a subsidiary of a large corporation which guaranteed the bonds. This reduced the lender's risk to a minimum, insuring a favorable rate. The bonds, with maturities ranging from 25 to 30 years, were issued at 6.9 percent. The issue size was approximately $5 million. Assuming that the corporation could have borrowed at prime, and rounding 6.9 to 7.0, the financing would have saved the corporation approximately $150,000 per year for the next 25 years. The savings would then have declined for the next five years as bonds mature.

A direct calculation would thus place the savings, in the 25-year period before the bonds mature, at $3.75 million ($150,000 × 25). A more sophisticated calculation, employing the present-value concept (see Appendix B), would place the savings at approximately $1.3 million, using a discount rate of 10 percent.

In this particular issue, the bonds were sold to the public through an underwriter, a procedure which is not worthwhile for smaller issues. Therefore, the buyers were not known to the development agency. Assume that the average buyer was in the 50 percent tax bracket. Had those same buyers lent the company an equivalent sum at the then-prevailing prime rate of 10 percent, interest payments would have totaled $500,000 per year, of which IRS would have taken $250,000. After-tax income for the buyers would thus have been $250,000 had they lent in the taxable market, rather than $350,000 (.07 × $5,000,000) in the tax-exempt market.

If one considers the federal government's annual tax expenditure to be the $250,000 in forgone taxes, the tax expenditure (implicit subsidy) is divided up as three-fifths going to the company and two-fifths to the bond buyers.

Obviously, there are some assumptions here, including one that the same sum would have been lent at prime in the taxable market. Therefore, one should not take the calculations too literally. But they do illustrate the general point that in tax-exempt financings, both the company and the lender receive an implicit subsidy from the federal government. The state of the markets, the creditworthiness of the firm, the tax status of the lenders, and the bargaining skills of borrower and lender will determine how this implicit subsidy is divided. Given that the utlimate intended beneficiary is, perhaps, a presently unemployed worker, the leakiness of the bucket in Okun's metaphor is evident.

Before going on, let us review a few salient points. The subsidy to the firm was a considerable one. A grant of the same size from EDA or HUD would be a substantial one that most local governments would be quite proud to have obtained. This implicit subsidy was obtained without the consent or consultation of the federal government. The agency determined it was in the interest of the municipality to fund the project, and the agency's bond counsel determined that under existing laws, the bonds would, in fact, have tax-exempt status. The bonds were issued and IRS was subsequently informed of their issuance.[3] The issuance of the bonds was a noncompetitive process. There was no finite amount of subsidy for which numerous projects had to compete. From the agency's point of view, the process was a simple one. The mechanics of the issue (which are not simple) were handled by the bond counsel and were paid off the top. Therefore, they were an expense met by the company. It is also an almost riskless transaction in that, in the event of default, neither the agency nor any unit of government will be liable to the bondholders.

For the agency, the size of the implicit subdidy and the manner in which it is divided up are of little interest because it is not the agency which is providing the subsidy. Even if the agency believes that there is a good possibility that the firm will go ahead with the project in any case, it is still worthwhile to offer the inducement on the chance that the inducement may be the deciding factor.

EDA PROGRAMS

The EDA, a branch of the Department of Commerce, was established in 1965 with the passage of the Public Works and Economic Development Act (PWEDA) of that year. It replaced the Area Redevelopment Administration, which had been established in 1961 to deal with poverty and structural unemployment, with so-called pockets of poverty, in rural areas. Although originally having a strong rural and small-town orientation, EDA has become active in urban areas as well in the last decade.

The focus on structural unemployment still remains at the core of EDA's congressional mandate, as the following citation from the PWEDA, as amended, indicates:

> The Congress declares that the maintenance of the national economy at a high level is vital to the best interests of the United States, but that some of our regions, counties, and communities are suffering substantial and persistent unemployment and underemployment; that such unemployment and underemployment cause hardship to many individuals and their families, and waste invaluable human resources; that to overcome this problem the Federal Government, in cooperation with the States, should help areas and regions of substantial and persistent unemployment and underemployment to take effective steps in planning and financing their public works and economic development; that Federal financial assistance, including grants for public works and development facilities to communities, industries, enterprises, and individuals in areas needing development should enable such areas to help themselves achieve lasting improvements and enhance the domestic prosperity by the establishment of stable and diversified local economies and improved local conditions . . . .

From the development agency's point of view, making use of EDA funding to promote local economic development is very different from the processes involved in tax-exempt financing. With the former, there is continuous involvement with government, the process is highly competitive, and a rather complicated local planning structure must be brought into being. In addition, there is the matter of local eligibility. Statistical criteria are used by EDA to determine which areas of the country are eligible for EDA funding. If the area has not been ruled eligible, EDA will not entertain a funding application from the area.

Several EDA programs will be described here in some detail and several others merely mentioned. For the agency seeking to use EDA funds, or even to determine if EDA funding should be sought, a detailed inquiry should be made at the office of the EDA economic development representative (EDR) for the state, at the EDA regional office, or at EDA headquarters in Washington, D.C. The following is just a preliminary sketch.

Most economic development assistance from EDA is authorized by the PWEDA of 1965. Of the act's ten titles, those listed below are of particular interest to economic developers. The other titles are either of an administrative nature or, in several cases, have never been funded.

- Title I: Grants for Public Works and Development Facilities
- Title II: Loans, Loan Guarantees, and Economic Development Revolving Fund
- Title III: Technical Assistance, Research, and Information
- Title IV: Area and District Eligibility
- Title IX: Special Economic Development and Adjustment Assistance

Title I is probably of most interest to economic developers. The title authorizes EDA to make direct grants for the acquisition or development of land and improvements for public works, public service, or development facility usage, and the acquisition, construction, rehabilitation, alteration, expansion, or improvement of such facilities, including related machinery and equipment. . . .

Grants may be to units of government and to private or public nonprofit organizations. Normally, the grants are 50-percent-matching ones, with the local government or nonprofit organization supplying the remainder of the funds. However, in areas showing a particularly high degree of economic distress, the federal share may go as high as 80 percent.

Eligibility and Application Procedures

The eligibility and application procedures require some explanation. Before EDA will consider a grant to an area, some criteria have to be met and a number of steps gone through.

Step one is the determination of area eligibility to receive EDA funding. To be eligible, an area must meet one of a number of statistical criteria. One of them is an unemployment rate of 6 percent or more for the last 12 months for which statistics are available. As of this writing, it is evident that by this criterion alone, much of the United States is eligible. Alternatively, a rate of 50 percent above the national rate for three of the past four years, or 75 percent above the national rate for two of the past three years, or double the national rate for one of the past two years, will suffice. Areas in which median family income is 50 percent or less of the national figure are also eligible. In addition, there are a number of other criteria of a somewhat more judgmental nature that may be used to render an area eligible. The details of these can be obtained from EDA and can also be found spelled out in the PWEDA as amended.[4]

In general, to be able to receive funding, or even to file a funding application, it is necessary for the political entity in question to become certified as a redevelopment area. In order to do this, the political entity must develop an overall economic development plan (OEDP). In order to write an OEDP, a committee which is broadly representative of the community must be set up. The committee must have minority representation at least in proportion to its percentage of total population; it must represent the poor; it must contain some public officials, some representatives of labor, some representatives of the business community. It is generally difficult to meet all of the committee-membership requirements with a group of less than 30.

This committee prepares the OEDP. The major elements in the OEDP are a statement about committee membership, an assessment of past development efforts (if any), a general description of the area and its economy, an assessment of the area's potential for economic development, a development strategy, and a plan for implementation.

When the OEDP is completed, it is submitted to EDA. If the plan is approved, the area is then certified as a redevelopment area and EDA will entertain applications for project funding.

Projects vary widely. Assume, for example, that a county which has been certified seeks to develop an industrial park. The plan is to use county-owned land that will be leased to industrial users under long-term leases. In order to develop the park, however, road access and storm drainage must be improved. Costs for this are estimated at $1 million. The county prepares an application for funding and submits it to EDA. If approved, EDA will normally fund half the cost, with the applicant responsible for the other half. Some of the applicant's share, but not an unduly large amount, may consist of services in kind (staff time, for instance).

The application will be judged on several points. One is its conformity with the OEDP. The project must fit into the development strategy of the OEDP. The project must have a reasonable chance of success. In this instance, evidence must be provided that if the site improvements are made, leases will be signed, structures erected, and permanent jobs created. The cost per job created is also considered. At present, EDA quotes a figure of $10,000 of EDA exposure per job created as a figure it does not like to exceed.

The agency will not fund projects in which it believes industry is being relocated from one area to another with the use of EDA funds, or where the project will create excess capacity in the area.

Although in the past, most applicants for EDA funding were counties and cities, EDA has recently encouraged the formation of economic development districts (EDDs). These are groups of counties, typically between five and ten. The OEDP process for them is similar to that described earlier. However, there are some differences. These are indicated by the following extract from an EDA publication:

> To get started, groups of adjacent counties with similar or related economic problems must first have the approval of the Governor to form a District. At least one of these counties must be a designated Redevelopment Area, eligible for Economic Development Administration grants and loans.
>
> There must also be a growth center—a city or center of economic activity that contains a population of not more than 250,000 and has the development potential to provide jobs and services for the Redevelopment Area unemployed or underemployed.
>
> If the District is to get moving, it must have a grassroots development board—an organization representative of area economic, political, civic and social interests.
>
> At least a majority of the board members will be local elected officials; one-third will be nongovernment people. The membership will include men and women from industry and labor, banking and business, farming and the professions, as well as representatives of

the unemployed. Minorities must be represented in proportion to their numbers, but not necessarily exceeding 25 percent.

The process has the advantage that EDA has indicated it will look with favor upon applications from such districts. Then, too, there is a 10 percent bonus on public works. That is, in the example given above EDS's share would be $600,000, rather than $500,000, if the application were from an EDD rather than a single county. There are, of course, some disadvantages, too, which will be mentioned shortly.

Advantages and Disadvantages of EDA Funding

Before discussing other EDA programs, let us consider the process described above. The requirement of an OEDP and of a broadly representative OEDP committee has advantages and disadvantages. For the area which has not previously engaged in serious economic planning, or which does not have a political establishment capable of doing serious thinking about economic questions, the act of creating the OEDP may be very useful. Even if no EDA funding is ever forthcoming, the carrot of funding may have impelled the community to begin a useful process. The requirement that the OEDP committee be broadly representative may be useful in building a base of support for whatever economic development efforts are ultimately forthcoming and also in seeing that the interests of many groups in the community are considered in the formulation of plans.

On the other hand, in a community in which previous economic or development planning has been done and in which the existing structure of government is already competent to do such planning, the OEDP process may be quite awkward. The OEDP committee, called into being to meet EDA requirements, may find itself either being something of a rubber stamp or in conflict with an established planning structure. Assume, for example, a development agency or a planning department has been working on the process of economic development for several years. The area becomes eligible for EDA funding, and it is decided to set up an OEDP committee to draft an OEDP and get the area certified. The possibilities for overlap and conflict with people already working and plans already in progress are evident.

In contrast to the tax-exempt-financing process, the quest for EDA funding is highly competitive. Many projects which meet the requirements described above will necessarily be turned down. The competitiveness of the process should not be underestimated. In fiscal 1979, EDA awarded $240 million in public-works grants, an average of $4.8 million per state. An average-size state in which economic development is a serious goal can readily come up with enough worthy projects to absorb many times that much money. In contrast to tax-exempt funding, the process involves extensive contact with government, beginning with OEDP formulation, and going through the various steps in the project application process.

From the development agency point of view, one problem with the use of EDA funding is the inability to give firms relatively quick answers. With tax-exempt funding, the economic developer can look at a proposal and offer a preliminary opinion on legality the same day. A more authoritative opinion can be obtained from the bond counsel in a period of a few days. Where a grant from an agency is required, the economic developer cannot speak for the granting agency. The best he can do is to describe the process to the firm and possibly offer a rough estimate on how long the wait for an answer will be. (The temptation to treat the possibility of a grant as a sure thing and thus hold on to the applicant may be strong, but in the long term such behavior leads to a loss of agency credibility.)

The EDD, as distinct from the single county, has both the advantages and disadvantages noted above. It also has some particular advantages and disadvantages. Economically, the EDD may make more sense than the single city or county, because it may be possible to choose a group of counties that form a natural economic entity. This is presumably one reason for EDA's preference for EDDs. The disadvantages appear to be largely political. The requirement that the EDD be approved by the state government inserts another, possibly time-consuming, step in the process. The requirement to designate a growth center in a multicounty group is also an obvious point at which conflict can occur. Questions of local pride, desire to claim political credit, and desire to enhance the local tax base all may cause the selection of a growth center to be a contentious process.

When all is said, however, the OEDP process and Title I of the PWEDA do permit a community to put together the financing to absorb front-end costs and thus stimulate private investment that would not otherwise occur.

It should be noted that EDA assistance can be combined with other types of financial assistance. In the example suggested earlier, tax-exempt financing for firms building on leased land might be used. The combination of EDA grant money absorbing a substantial part of the front-end site costs and tax-exempt funding lowering the cost of construction could be a very powerful combination. If the firms building in the park were not strong enough to obtain conventional credit strictly on their own, loans or loan guarantees from the Small Business Administration (SBA), or second-mortgage financing from a state or the local development agency might be considered.

Title II of the PWEDA

Title II of the PWEDA authorizes EDA to make loans and to guarantee loans to a variety of entities including businesses, nonprofit organizations, political entities, Indian tribes, and private lending institutions. In general, EDA loans and loan guarantees are made in economic redevelopment areas or in economic development districts. Thus, getting certified as a redevelopment area makes firms within the area eligible for EDA loans and loan guarantees.

Loan guarantees may extend to up to 90 percent of the value of the loan. In this regard, they are similar to SBA guarantees (discussed subsequently), but they do not have a fixed upper limit while SBA guarantees do. While the interest on EDA guaranteed loans is not specified, an agency publication notes:

> Interest rates on EDA-guaranteed loans by private lending institutions must be consistent with the marketplace. However, EDA recognizes that its 90-percent guarantee substantially reduces the risk to a lender. Consequently, EDA requires that the interest charged by a lender in a 90-percent guaranteed loan be in close relationship to that charged to preferred customers: proportionately higher rates will ordinarily result in proportionately lower guarantees.

Direct loans by EDA to firms on fixed assets may extend to up to 65 percent and loans for working capital may be up to the full amount required. Terms may extend to 25 years on fixed-asset loans and to five years on working-capital loans. EDA has various requirements regarding equity participation and/or subordinated loans. EDA also requires that the loan application be approved by a state or local agency directly concerned with economic development. Total exposure is generally limited to $10,000 per job saved or created (as cited before). Finally, EDA loans and loan guarantees will be available only where other sources of financing are not available under conditions which make the project feasible.

The process is a highly competitive one. Applications will exceed EDA's capacity to lend and guarantee by a considerable margin. The economic developer encouraging or assisting a firm in seeking an EDA loan or loan guarantee should be aware that in addition to the competitive nature of the process, the time required for processing the application will be substantially longer than with a commercial lender. As is also true in regard to tax-exempt financing, the economic developer should advise the firm that his dealings with EDA may constitute a public record available to any interested party under freedom-of-information laws.

Title III

Title III of the PWEDA enables EDA to provide technical assistance either directly or in the form of funding for staff, consultant services, and other project-study expenses. Where EDA provides direct assistance, as much as 100 percent of the cost may be assumed by EDA. In other instances EDA funding is generally limited to 75 percent. However, in both these connections, EDA notes that it seeks maximum possible financial participation by the applicant. Although EDA notes that most technical assistance grants will go to redevelopment areas, EDDs, or growth centers, grants may go to other areas under some circumstances. Among the circumstances which might permit this are close links between the economy of the grant applicant and a designated area, imminent shut-down of a major source of employment, and economic problems leading to severe unemployment or economic distress within a part of a larger area (such as an impoverished area of a large city).

As with all EDA funding, the application process is competitive. The application process, which involves description of the area, relationship of the project study to other economic planning efforts, a description of all work to be performed, research techniques to be used, requires that a certain amount of groundwork be done before the jurisdiction is in a position to apply for technical assistance. Very often EDA technical assistance takes the form of feasibility studies for specific projects.

Title IV

Title IV of the PWEDA sets forth the bases for area eligibility, as noted before. As of September 30, 1979, 2,575 areas in the United States were qualified for EDA financial assistance.[5] EDA lists the bases for qualification, and areas that qualify, as follows:

Basis	Number of Areas
Persistent unemployment	230
Median family income	86
Indian reservations	176
Sudden rise in unemployment	47
Special-impact areas	365
Per capita employment	114
Substantial unemployment	1,556
One redevelopment area per state	1

Thus, depth and/or chronicity of unemployment are the main reasons for area eligibility. EDA notes that, using 1976 population estimates, eligible areas contain a population of 167,500,000. In 1976 the population of the United States was estimated at about 215 million, so that approximately 80 percent of the U.S. population lived in eligible areas. Given increases in unemployment from the recession, beginning in the spring of 1980, it is likely that the percentage is now higher.

From the viewpoint of the economic developer seeking sources of development capital, the overall shape of EDA funding is of little concern. His only interest is whether his area is eligible and whether the chances for funding appear to justify the effort required to pursue the matter. From a broader perspective, the wide eligibility raises questions as to whether there is a strong overall direction to the investment of public funds in economic development. This question can also be raised, and with even greater force, with regard to tax-exempt financing. Not only is that available almost ubiquitously, but because of the non-competitive nature of the process, relative degrees of need do not figure into the distribution of benefits.

Title IX

Title IX provides grant money for areas which either have experienced sudden economic dislocation (for example, the closing of a major employer) or whose economy faces the prospect of long-term deterioration. In fiscal 1979, EDA expended slightly less than $86 million on this category. Approximately $45 million was spent in areas characterized by long-term deterioration and almost $41 million for sudden-dislocation grants. Funds are available for a wide range of activities including planning, public works, business loans, acquisition and renovation of structures. In order to obtain funding under Title IX, an area must demonstrate that its conditions do meet the particular meaning of this title. Even if the area has completed an OEDP and been certified as a redevelopment area, it must still be separately designated as eligible for Title IX assistance.

In addition to programs authorized by the PWEDA (1965) as amended, EDA has from time to time administered other programs. The 1976 and 1978 rounds of countercyclical public-works grants (local public works) were administered by EDA. Municipalities filed project applications with EDA, which used statistical and other criteria to allocate funds.

Under the Trade Act of 1974, firms whose business has been adversely affected by increased imports can apply to EDA for assistance. If the firm meets statutory requirements for certification under this program, it is eligible for loans and loan guarantees that may be used for the acquisition or improvement of capital assets or for working capital. Again, the process is competitive and certification does not automatically guarantee that assistance will be forthcoming. In fiscal 1979, EDA loans, loan guarantees, and technical assistance grants in this area totaled approximately $116 million.

On occasion, EDA may engage in special projects, outside its usual run of activities. In 1979 its special steel program, created at the request of the president, guaranteed approximately $343 million in loans to the steel industry. Although the loan guarantees are authorized under Title II, the size of the loans was vastly greater than is common for EDA. For example, a single loan guarantee of $111 million was made on behalf of Jones & Laughlin Steel Corp.

HUD GRANTS

With the passage of the Housing and Community Development Act of 1977 (section 110 of Title I), the Department of Housing and Urban Development has been empowered to make urban development action grants (UDAGs) to promote economic development in urban areas.[6]

These grants differ from community development (CD) grants in a number of ways. Unlike CD grants, they are completely discretionary. There is no entitlement to UDAG funds. Additional, UDAG funds may be made available only to communities which exhibit certain statistical indicators of distress. Thus, many communities which are entitled to CD funds are not eligible to apply for UDAG funds.

UDAG funding differs from EDA funding in certain important regards. Most important, from a political standpoint, it does not require the establishment of a separate planning function. The application is submitted by the municipality. Another distinction is that UDAG funds can be used for some purposes not directly tied to economic development and, on the other hand, the application for UDAG funding will be judged partly on the effort the community has made in regard to some noneconomic goals.

Eligibility criteria vary somewhat by place size, primarily because the types of data commonly available for municipalities vary by size.

For cities with over 50,000 and for urban communities, eligibility is attained by meeting three of the following six criteria:

- per capita income—a net increase between 1969 and 1974 of $1,424 or less
- population growth—15.52 percent or smaller from 1960 to 1975
- unemployment rate—7.69 percent or greater for 1976
- employment growth—7.08 percent or smaller in manufacturing and retailing between 1967 and 1972
- housing stock—34.15 percent of it or more constructed prior to 1940
- poverty-level group—11.24 percent or more of city's population

In the relatively unlikely event that the percentage of the area's population under the federal poverty level should be less than half specified above, the municipality will be required to qualify under four of the remaining five criteria.

If the community's percentage of population under the federal poverty line is more than one and one-half times that of all metropolitan cities, and if its per capita income figure is below the median, then it may be able to establish a unique distress factor. For example, the loss of a major employer or a shift in technology obsoleting a major industry might be judged to be a unique distress factor if the two conditions mentioned above are met. Note, however, that meeting these statistical criteria does not alone establish the distress factor. For cities between 25,000 and 50,000 in population, the above list of criteria is modified by taking out the unemployment item. The city must then meet four of the remaining five criteria. For cities between 2,500 and 25,000, the list is reduced to four by taking out the employment-growth criterion as well. These communities must meet three of the four criteria.

HUD regulations also specify that eligibility is contingent upon community efforts and low- and moderate-income housing:

In order to qualify, the applicant must demonstrate that it has achieved reasonable results in providing housing for persons of low and moderate income. Among the factors HUD will consider are the number of federally or other assisted housing units provided for low- and moderate-income households, especially since 1974. Specifically, HUD will evaluate the applicant's activities in implementing the proportional goals established in any HUD-approved Housing Assistance Plan applicable to the applicant's jurisdiction. . . .

Note that there are no comparable explicit requirements to be met for EDA funding.

HUD regulations specify several criteria for the weighing of projects, once an area's eligibility has been established. The above extract, as well as those that follow, are from the *Federal Register* for January 10, 1978, Part IV, and October 25, 1977, Part III. As the "primary criterion," HUD lists "the comparative degree of physical and economic distress," which shall be ascertained as follows (decimals indicate the relative weight to be accorded each factor):

1. the percentage of the area's total housing stock that was built prior to 1940: .5;
2. the percentage of its total current population that was in poverty in 1970: .3; and
3. the degree to which its population growth rate lags behind that of all metropolitan cities: .2.

Note that the weighting accorded items 1 and 3 should favor older urban areas. Only item 2 is a direct indicator of distresses experienced by individuals.

Another criterion of some interest in HUD regulations is the "impact of the proposed project on the special problems of low- and moderate-income persons and minorities." Again, this is an idea which finds no comparison in EDA criteria, though it might be argued that EDA's area-eligibility criteria of unemployment and personal income have somewhat the same intent.

Of particular significance, HUD indicates that the extent of financial participation by "private entities" and by state and other "public entities" will also influence its evaluation of the project. One term which came into prominence in the Carter administration, with regard to the federal financing of local economic development, is "leveraging," i.e., the ratio of federal to total funds committed. All other things being equal, the more highly leveraged the project, the more favorably it will be viewed. The desire to achieve maximum leveraging is entirely understandable from the federal point of view, for the highly leveraged project affords a greater return per federal dollar. Secondarily, the fact that a high degree of leverage can be achieved suggests a higher degree of investor confidence and therefore argues a higher expectation of project success. The reader may reflect, however, that there is an inherent contradiction between the use of distress as a criterion and the use of leveraging as a criterion. For the more distressed the area, the less likely it is to attract large amounts of private capital and the more difficult it will be for it to achieve a high degree of leverage. This sort of contradiction is hardly unique to UDAGs. In a general sense, the question of whether development assistance is directed to areas most in need or to areas where the chance of success is greatest is one with which any economic development effort is likely to have to wrestle.

Finally, as is to be expected, project feasibility is an important criterion. HUD indicates that it will consider

> the feasibility of accomplishing the project in a timely fashion within the total resources which will be provided. HUD will consider such factors as the status of land assembly and zoning, the environmental status of the project, and the administrative and legal mechanisms for accomplishing the project. Proposals will be considered to have a lesser degree of feasibility if they involve substantial additional planning, lengthy start-up time, or are subject to such potential obstacles as environmental or legal constraints.

HUD notes that awards will be made 60 to 90 days after the application has been submitted (i.e., in the same quarter). However, it also notes that even though an award is made, no funding will be received until an environmental assessment is completed and legally binding private financial commitments have been made.

Several points regarding UDAG funding should be noted briefly. Projects funded by UDAGs must be in keeping with other community development goals and they must be subject to A95 review (a process in which a regional agency reviews them for consistency with regional development goals). Project applications must also demonstrate that there has been adquate citizen participation, "with special attention to measures to encourage moderate-income persons, minorities, and residents of blighted neighborhoods . . ."

Essentially, UDAG moneys may be used for the same activities as community development block grant (CDBG) funds. "Basic eligible activities" include:

- acquisition of land and structures, including air rights, water rights;
- disposition of the above;
- public-facilities improvements;
- clearance activities;
- public services;
- interim assistance (this might be repair of streets, removal of debris, snow removal);
- payment of nonfederal share in connection with a federal grant-in-aid program;
- urban-renewal completion;

• relocation payments to individuals or businesses;
• loss of rental-income payments;
• removal of architectural barriers.

Under "eligible economic development activities," HUD specifically lists "acquisition of real property for economic development"; "acquisition, construction, reconstruction, rehabilitation, or installation of public facilities" not otherwise eligible under the basic "eligible activities" listing; "acquisition, construction, reconstruction, rehabilitation, or installation of commercial or industrial buildings." This latter item includes a substantial variety of diverse activities including energy conservation and real property improvements, such as rail spurs.

In addition to the above, UDAG funds may be used to finance small business investment companies (SBICs) and for a variety of assistance to local businesses, including working capital; capital for land, structures, and property improvement; obtaining of performance bonding for minority contractors.

Beyond all of the above, funds may be used for housing rehabilitation and preservation and for a variety of planning purposes. It appears, to date, that UDAG funds have largely been used for land assembly and writedown and for infrastructure development, activities which have been common to urban-renewal and community development programs in the past. UDAGs are relatively new and it may be that with the passage of time, distinct patterns of funding will emerge. Though the above will give the reader a general conception of the UDAG program, it is not meant as a complete summary. More details are available from the *Federal Register* and from HUD.

The UDAG procedure differs from the EDA procedure for the OEDP in a number of ways. The largest difference, from a political viewpoint, as noted before, is the lack of the requirement for a separate planning process. This should make the UDAG process easier in that the time spent in assembling the OEDP committee and in formulating the OEDP will not be necessary. It should also, as noted before, void the problem of conflict and awkwardness arising between a special committee and an established planning and development structure. Whether the requirements for a demonstrated record on low- and moderate-income housing will rule out the use of UDAG funding for some communities remains to be seen. Similarly, the effects of public participation requirements, with their special emphasis on low- and moderate-income people, may or may not pose problems for some communities. In a complex, densely developed area, it is hard to do anything of consequence without creating some legitimate claim of injury.

SMALL BUSINESS ADMINISTRATION (SBA) PROGRAMS

SBA operates a number of programs through which firms can obtain debt and, in some instances, equity financing. More often than not, the economic developer will not be directly involved in those programs, but it is well for him to have some acquaintance with them so that he can guide firms to them.

In general, SBA programs are oriented to firms which cannot obtain financing through conventional channels. In an area whose economy is stagnant or declining, SBA funding programs may be of particular value in keeping existing firms going. In general, SBA funding is geared to the smaller firms. The firm which can obtain tax-exempt financing is a firm which could not meet the SBA loan criterion of inability to obtain conventional financing. Conversely, the firm which is eligible for SBA funding would not have the credit rating to satisfy potential buyers of tax-exempt bonds.

In short, much SBA funding is complementary to other types of funding previously discussed. Only a few of the SBA programs, those of particular interest to economic developers, are discussed below. SBA financing is available only to businesses considered to be small. For manufacturers, this generally means employment not exceeding the 250-to-1,500 range, depending upon the field. For wholesalers, it means yearly sales from $9.2 million to $22 million, depending upon the field; for retailing, from $2 million to $7.5 million, again depending upon the particular field. Comparable service-industry figures are $2-to-$8 million. For general contractors, the limit is annual receipts not exceeding $9.5 million. In addition to the above limits, SBA also requires that the firm not be dominant in its field and that it first be refused conventional credit. To establish refusal, a letter from one or more banks indicating that credit has been denied is usually accepted as evidence.

SBA business loans and guarantees take two forms.[7] First, SBA will obligate itself to purchase 90 percent of a bank loan if the borrower is more than 90 days in default. By thus reducing the bank's exposure to 10 percent of the face amount of the loan, banks are induced to make loans which could not be justified under conventional criteria. Second, direct loans are generally made only when the above possibility has been exhausted.

SBA loan guarantees extend to up to $350,000 and to 90 percent of the loan amount, whichever is smaller. If it can be shown that the loan will be used in a manner that meets some defined national priority (air pollution control, energy conservation, improvement of balance of trade), SBA may be willing to extend the $350,000 ceiling to as high as $500,000.

For loan guarantees, the firm works through a bank. The bank, in fact, may be the one which has turned the firm down for conventional credit. The SBA loan guarantee offers the bank the advantage of up to a 90 percent reduction in exposure. On the other hand, the process does impose additional effort and paperwork on the bank. Thus, some banks are interested in SBA guaranteed loans and some are not. For the firm seeking an SBA guaranteed loan, the first task is to locate an interested bank.

For SBA direct loans, the firm approaches the regional office of the SBA directly. Direct loans are currently limited to $150,000 as a matter of administrative ruling, with interest rates (as of mid-1980) of 8¼ percent. Thus, the SBA rate is several points below prime on a loan which conventional lenders consider too risky to make—obviously, extremely advantageous financing.

SBA loans and loan guarantees may be used for a wide variety of purposes including plant construction, improvements, purchase of equipment, and working capital. There are a limited number of uses to which they cannot be put, including speculative activities, and acquisition of property for resale.

The local development corporation (LDC) making use of SBA loans and loan guarantees is of considerable interest to the economic developer. This is particularly so for the economic developer working in a distressed area where availability of credit is a major problem.

The LDC is defined by SBA as

any corporation which: (a) is formed by public spirited citizens interested in planned economic growth of a community, with at least 75 percent ownership and control held by persons living or doing business in the community; (b) has been incorporated either for profit or non-profit under laws of the State in which it expects to do business; (c) is authorized to promote and assist the growth and development of small businesses in its area of operations; and (d) has a minimum of 25 stockholders or members.

It can provide capital for small firms in a variety of ways. These include loans to the firm for constructing and equipping facilities, purchase of the facility with lease-back to firm, with or without an option to buy, and sale of the completed facility to firm.

In the typical financing, a small percentage of the total comes directly from the LDC while the major portions come from SBA and a participating local bank. The SBA share is a maximum of $500,000 per participating business (the same LDC may capitalize many businesses) at a rate established annually by SBA. The loan from the bank is at a reasonable, i.e., market, rate and may be guaranteed by SBA to the extent of 90 percent or $500,000, whichever is less. SBA may take a second position on its loan, thus giving the private institution the security of holding the first lien. SBA loans through LDCs cannot be made if other sources of credit are available. They cannot be made for working capital and, in general, cannot be used for refinancing. The loans are secured by liens on fixed assets and may also be secured by other instruments including personal guarantees of principals.

The process will lower the firm's debt service because the SBA portion of the financing is below market interest rates (8¼ percent in mid-1980), and because of the reduced risk for the private lender. But the most important aspect of the process is that it makes financing possible at all.

Given the legal requirements of the LDC, such an organization cannot be part of a governmental development program. However, a government economic development agency might take steps to encourage the formation of such a group privately and then maintain a close working relationship with it. A non-governmental development organization might constitute itself as an LDC or might contain an LDC as part of its legal structure.

Another SBA-based process of which the economic developer should be aware, primarily to be able to refer firms to it, involves the small business investment corporation (SBIC).[8] Each dollar of private capital the SBIC is able to raise can be matched by up to $4 borrowed from the federal financing bank (FFB) under SBA guarantees. Unlike the case with many other SBA programs, the firm which borrows from, or receives equity financing from, an SBIC does not need to demonstrate inability to obtain financing from other sources. It should also be noted that SBIC loans are not necessarily cheap money. SBA permits the SBIC to charge up to 7 percent above the federal financing bank rate (i.e., the rate at which the SBIC borrows). In July 1980 the FFB rate on ten-year money was approximately 10.2 percent so that the cost to the borrowing firm might have been 17.2 percent. From the economic developer's point of view, the importance of the SBIC is that it is an important source of venture capital to which he can refer firms. A list of SBICs can be obtained from the SBA regional office. A selected list of SBICs, as well as other sources of venture capital, can be found in a study by Smollen and Hayes.[9] SBICs serving minority firms operate under rules similar, but not identical, to other SBICs. At one time, they were referred to as MESBICs (minority-enterprise small business investment corporations). This term has been dropped and they are now referred to as section 301(d) SBICs.

In addition to the above, there are a number of other SBA programs which the economic developer should be familiar with primarily for referral purposes. These include disaster loans (both physical and economic), loans related to energy conservation, loans to contractors.

NOTES

1. Section 103(b) (6) (d).

2. If the bonds are to be used for pollution control or waste disposal, there is no upper limit on the size of the issue.

3. The document informing IRS of the financing and informing IRS that the financing is made pursuant to certain provisions of the IRS code is referred to as a "statement of election," i.e., electing to be treated under the except-small-issues provisions noted earlier.

4. 42 U.S.C. 3121.

5. Communication with EDA. Comparable figures for earlier years can be obtained from EDA annual reports.

6. PL 95-128.

7. In the early 1970s, joint-participation loans between a bank and SBA were made. Apparently, for reasons of administrative complexity, these are no longer made.

8. This program is authorized by Section 502 of the Small Business Investment Act of 1958. The loans are generally referred to as "502 loans."

9. Leonard E. Smollen, John Hayes, et al., *Sources of Capital for Community Economic Development*, Center for Community Economic Development, Cambridge, 1976.

11

MANPOWER PLANNING

More often than not, manpower planning and economic development are separate functions handled by separate agencies. Their sources of funding are usually different and often they are divided by a difference in perspective. Manpower programs and planners are largely client oriented. Their primary goal is to serve those least able to compete on their own in the labor market. Conversely, the economic developer is likely to be firm oriented. While the manpower planner may, in the extreme, think of the firm as a device for providing jobs to his clients, the economic developer at the other extreme may think of labor simply as another input the firm requires. If skilled workers are available in abundance and wages are relatively low, the economic developer will describe the labor market as "good" in his conversations with prospective firms. The same market, viewed by the manpower planner, may be a disaster. Buyer and seller are not likely to view the same market in the same way.

Yet in spite of the differences in perspective, and sometimes in loyalties, there is room for cooperation between manpower and economic development efforts. The better the match between the labor needs of new and expanding firms and the skills and experience of the local labor force, the more the economic development will benefit the resident population. The economic developer, by shaping the development program, and the manpower planner, by shaping training and work-experience programs, can strive toward making the match as good as possible. To the extent that manpower programs improve manpower quality, the efforts of the manpower planner may strengthen the hand of the economic developer in his recruitment and retention efforts. Finally, and not to be ignored, manpower-training programs do offer a number of financial carrots to firms—useful information for the economic developer to have when the inevitable "What can you do for us?" arises.

This chapter is intended to acquaint the economic developer with current manpower-training programs and policies as well as with some of the vocabulary of the field; the last section of the chapter defines a few of the terms used.

A BRIEF HISTORY OF MANPOWER PLANNING

Until the Great Depression, manpower planning and manpower programs, as they are known today, did not exist in the United States. With the Great Depression, the need for job creation became apparent and federal moneys were quickly allocated to this end. By the end of 1933, the first year of the Roosevelt administration, over 4 million Americans were employed in federally funded jobs, a huge figure for a population little more than half its present size.[1]

The problem to be dealt with was clearly that of cyclical unemployment and the person to be helped was, by and large, the male head of household with some prior work experience. The present manpower concept of targeting assistance at particular segments of the population was absent. Today's manpower vocabulary, with terms like "structural unemployment," "pockets of poverty," the "economically disadvantaged," and "underemployment," did not exist. It was not that the factual basis for these terms did not exist, but rather, that the fact of massive cyclical unemployment was overwhelming.

Job creation as a major role of the federal government lasted through the 1930s and then became superfluous with the macroeconomic stimulus provided by the coming of World War II. The Work Projects Administration (WPA) was formally ended in 1943, having lost its reason for being perhaps two years earlier.[2]

The single most worrisome economic question facing the nation during the war was whether, after the reconversion period was over, the nation would be able to avoid sinking back into the stagnation of the 1930s. Coincidentally, Keynesian economic theory had first been unveiled during the Great Depression. (Keynes published *The General Theory of Employment, Interest and Money* in 1936.) By the time the war ended, Keynesian theory had become widely accepted within the economics profession. It dominated macroeconomic policy after the war. The very success of Keynesian macroeconomic policy during the 15 years or so after World War II served both to reduce and to mask the needs for manpower policy and programs. Though it is now commonplace to despair of Keynesian economics because of the apparent inability of governments to deal simultaneously with the dual problems of unemployment and inflation in the 1970s, Keynesian macroeconomic policy was in fact highly successful in the late 1940s and 1950s. Except for brief periods of inflation in 1945–46, and again at the beginning of the Korean War, inflation was trivial by today's standards. Unemployment was relatively low, and real per capita GNP rose at the rate of several percent a year. A comparison of the 15 years after 1918 with the 15 years after 1945 offered strong evidence that the age of the economist had, indeed, arrived.

Given the success of postwar macroeconomic policy, there was a general feeling that the main task of government was to maintain aggregate demand at a level sufficiently high to guarantee full employment. As one writer notes, the labor force was visualized as being like a queue arranged from the most productive to least productive. The greater the demand for labor, the further down the queue employers would go in hiring.[3] The way to help those at the end of the queue was to stimulate aggregate demand and hence the derived demand for labor. This view was expressed in President Kennedy's inaugural address by the phrase "A rising tide lifts all the boats."

But in spite of the general postwar prosperity, it gradually became apparent that the entire society did not seem to partake of the general prosperity. "Pockets of poverty" seemed to persist year after year. Structural unemployment could exist in the face of sustained high employment and general prosperity. In the late 1950s, pressures for programs targeted both at individuals and at places mounted. The formation of the Area Redevelopment Administration in 1961 was noted in Chapter 10. On the manpower side of the issue, the pressure culminated in the passage of the Manpower Development and Training Act (MDTA) in 1962. Underlying the act was the premise that there existed a mismatch between the needs of employers and the skills of workers. The major thrust of the act, as originally passed, was to provide living expenses for heads of households while they went through job-training programs to acquire new skills. The program appealed both to liberals who had been pushing for manpower programs and to conservatives who saw the bill as a way to reduce relief and unemployment rolls, increase productivity, and perhaps even shift the Phillips curve in a favorable direction.[4]

Shortly after the act was passed and funding begun, the so-called Kennedy tax cut was initiated and unemployment rates began to decline, reaching about 4 percent by the end of 1965. Unemployment rates among male heads of households—the primary targets of the MDTA—fell to very low levels. But other problems became apparent. Youth unemployment, fueled partly by the entrance of large numbers of young people born in the early years of the baby boom, and partly by economic stagnation in many urban areas, became a national issue. The MDTA was extended through a series of amendments that gradually restructured it into a broad-based manpower bill with youth programs, residential-training programs, on-the-job training, vocational education.

The MDTA, as amended, remained the mainstay of federal manpower policy until the passage of the Comprehensive Employment and Training Act (CETA) at the end of 1973.

CETA, also amended several times, is the central basis of federal manpower policy and funding. CETA departed from former manpower policy significantly in that it shifted decision making and administrative responsibility from the federal government to local government. Not only has responsibility for running programs and expanding funds been shifted away from Washington, but the local governments have been given considerable discretion regarding the activities upon which moneys can be expended and the clients for whom they may be expended. The buzzwords at the time of the passage of CETA were "decentralization" and "decategorization." Uneuphonious as they are, they accurately described the direction in which the passage of CETA moved federal manpower policy.[5]

At the center of the CETA administrative structure is the prime sponsor, a local government or a consortium of local governments with a population of 100,000 or more.[6] The prime sponsor receives federal funding on the basis of a formula based on unemployment and poverty. It creates a manpower planning council, which sets manpower policy. Within the broad limits of CETA, localities have substantial freedom in the allocation of funds. Where such major elements of the program as training are contracted out, the contract is between prime sponsor and vendor.

Since its inception, the program has gone through several phases. In the first period, there was an emphasis on training. But, with the deepening of the recession in 1975 and early 1976, the emphasis shifted to job creation. A large number of municipalities used CETA funding to hire former employees who could not be carried on the municipal payroll and to supplement salaries of regular employees.

In 1977, the job-creation role of CETA was strengthened further with the passage of the Economic Stimulus Appropriations Act (PL 95-29) which provided the funding to more-than-double public service employment (PSE), to 725,000 jobs.[7]

In 1978, CETA was substantially amended.[8] The new CETA, as the amended law has been referred to, differs from previous versions largely in its greater emphasis on targeting CETA funds at those who would have, and have had, the most difficulty in the labor market. Ray Marshall, then secretary of labor, noted:

> *CETA funds have not been clearly aimed at those who need help the most.* The previous Administrations used CETA as a form of backdoor revenue sharing. In some cases, CETA funds were used to shift city workers from local to federal payrolls. Architects and city planners were kept on the payroll through CETA funds ostensibly designed to help the disadvantaged. Local governments could supplement CETA dollars without any limit, and, as a result, some CETA workers were middle-class professionals.[9]

Of course, many mayors and county supervisors might counter that they indeed did use CETA funds in the manner alleged, and that had they not been able to do so, municipal services would have suffered severely. There is no question that the public administrator using CETA funds to hire was often torn between the desire to help those most needing help and the desire to hire the most competent available person. It would not be surprising if the latter motivation won out in the majority of cases. In any event, the new CETA is distinguished from the old CETA largely by its stipulations with regard to eligibility for PSE and for training. One can also see in the new eligibility requirements an intent to use CETA training and job creation to pull people out of dependence on public assistance.

A brief summary of the various titles of CETA follows.[10]

Title	Approximate Funding in FY 1980 (figures in millions)	Description
I	—	This title sets forth general provisions applicable to the act. Of particular interest, it establishes criteria for participation in CETA programs: no one can be in any CETA program longer than 2½ years in a five-year period; and no one can be in PSE longer than 78 weeks in a five-year period. There also is a waiver for on-board enrollees, at the department secretary's discretion, if a prime sponsor is having extreme hardship in placing PSE enrollees in unsubsidized jobs, or if the area has 7 percent or more unemployment. PSE wages may not exceed $10,000 per year, adjusted upward by the ratio that local wage rates bear to the national average, but not to exceed 20 percent of the maximum (no more than $12,000), with some exceptions. Further, average wages in each prime-sponsor area may not exceed $7,200, adjusted by the ratio that local wages bear to the national average.
II B and C	2,054 1,485 3,539	Provides for a variety of "training, education, work experience, upgrading, retraining and other services," and "counterstructural public service employment." Titles IIB and C relate to training

Title	Approximate Funding in FY 1980 (figures in millions)	Description
		for employment and upgrading of skills for the employed. IID relates to the provision of counter-structural* PSE. Participants in most of the training programs and services must be "economically disadvantaged" and "unemployed, underemployed, or in school." Participants in PSE must be economically disadvantaged and unemployed for more than 15 weeks or on welfare.
III	536	Special federal responsibilities: programs for persons who have a particular disadvantage in the labor market, including native Americans, migrants, and other seasonal farmworkers, the handicapped, women, displaced homemakers, public assistance recipients, and other special-target groups. Authorizes welfare demonstration projects, projects for middle-aged and older workers, and a program for better coordination between prime sponsors and state employment security agencies. Voucher demonstration projects are now mandated.
IV	1,850	A variety of youth programs for employment and training; includes Job Corps (a residential training program) and summer employment programs.
V		"Renames and reconstitutes the National Commission on Manpower Policy." Not a funded program.
VI	1,627	Countercyclical Public Service Employment Program. Provides funding for public service employment when the national unemployment rate exceeds 4 percent. Jobs are to be provided to employ 20 percent of the unemployed in excess of 4 percent unless unemployment rises to 7 percent, in which case the figure rises to 25 percent. Because of its countercyclical role, eligibility requirements are somewhat more flexible than for the counterstructural program.

---

*"Counterstructural" means programs designed to counteract structural employment. Eligibility standards are somewhat more strict than for the countercyclical funding under Title VI.

Title	Approximate Funding in FY 1980 (figures in millions)	Description
VII	325	This title authorizes a Private Sector Initiative Program (PSIP) to increase private-sector involvement in both training and employment. It provides for the establishment of private industry councils (PICs), a majority of whose members must be from the business community, which shall participate with prime sponsors in developing opportunities for economically disadvantaged persons in the private sector.
VIII	250	Young Adult Conservation Corps. Work experience for young adults on "conservation and other projects on federal lands and waters."
Total	8,127	

From the economic developer's point of view, several CETA titles are of interest. Titles IIB and C could be used to fund training programs, practical or classroom, that prepare workers for private-sector employment. Training expenditures funded through CETA could be combined with other efforts to bring in jobs and tighten the local labor market. For example, tax abatements, industrial revenue bonds, and mortgage guarantees might be used to lower the costs of constructing a plant. A CETA training program might then be used to improve the reading, mathematical, mechanical, or other skills of prospective employees. In addition, CETA funds might be used for on-the-job training at the new plant. Under this program, up to half of the wage costs of eligible workers can be paid by CETA during the length of the training program, a time period which varies with the nature of the job skills being taught.

Both the counterstructural and countercyclical provisions of CETA might be used to provide public-sector employment that would equip CETA workers with skills needed by private-sector employers. Comparable comments might be made with regard to Titles III and IV. To the extent that CETA expenditures can improve manpower quality and shift training costs from employers to the public fisc, they may be used as an inducement to locate in (or remain in or expand in) the jurisdiction.

The above is not to minimize the difficulties of matching public manpower efforts to the needs of employers or to the actions of an economic development program. Nor is it to minimize the difficulty of getting employers to look with favor upon CETA-funded programs as desirable sources of labor. To be quite blunt about it, many employers perceive the work force offered them by the public sector as a low-quality one. It is almost pointless to argue whether the perception is accurate, for it is the fact of the perception which is central.

The new CETA, with its well-intentioned emphasis on aiding those most needing help, may make the economic development uses of CETA more difficult ones by strengthening employers' fears regarding labor-force quality. This is hardly a criticism of the direction of the new CETA, for it is hard to imagine that anyone familiar with the old CETA could fail to recognize the truth of Marshall's comments quoted previously. It is simply that a program targeted at those least able to function on their own in the labor market will not be perceived by employers as a source of high-quality manpower.

As an economic development tool, some state programs may be far more successful than federal programs because they are oriented to employers' needs and do not impose the sorts of restrictions on eligibility that CETA does. In South Carolina, for example, the State Board for Technical and Comprehensive Education operates a technical education program for firms moving into the state. The state negotiates with firms prior to the start of their operations and designs training programs to be conducted by state technical schools. The programs, which are essentially costless to the firm, are tailored to the firm's needs. Participants may be selected by the board or by the prospective employer. They receive training free, but are not paid for participating in the program. Though it is expected that program graduates will be hired by the employer, the firm is not legally obligated to do so. The employer loses no control over his hiring process. In contrast to CETA, there are no unemployment or family income-status requirements. From the employer's point of view, the program is very attractive. The training is tailored to his production needs. The fact that trainees are not paid for participating and are not selected on a needs basis assuages any doubts about labor-force quality. In fact, participation in the program is likely to be taken by the employer as a sign of strong motivation on the part of the potential employee.

The contrast between the state program and CETA is very clear. CETA, particularly the new CETA, is targeted at the most needful, with the hope that there will be some transfer to private-sector employment. The South Carolina program makes no effort at targeting, but instead, is structured to meet employer needs.

If one is interested in the relationship between program structure and underlying political reality, one might note that the South Carolina constitution contains a right-to-work provision, and that about 7 percent of its nonagricultural labor force is unionized, the lowest such figure in the nation.

MANPOWER PLANNING

The CETA program, and MDTA before it, largely brought into being a new profession—manpower planning. The discussion which follows is largely adapted from practice that has developed in connection with federal funding. That practice is obviously client rather than employer oriented.

A federal guide for manpower planning lists the following steps in the process:[11]

- Define program purpose.
- Develop area analysis.
- Define needs.
- Establish priorities.
- Inventory and assess current programming efforts.
- Establish goals.
- Set initial objectives.
- Design an initial participant-service system.
- Detail the capacity of the initial client-service system.
- Identify and describe necessary administrative and management support services.
- Design an initial organization and staffing plan.
- Estimate costs.
- Develop initial work statements.
- Develop detailed cost estimates.
- Determine program operators.
- Develop a final detailed operational plan.
- Prepare CETA application and submit it for review.
- Implement the plan and take action.
- Use the plan to manage the program.

Without going through the above steps singly, let us consider a few main points. The first half-dozen steps involve a study of the labor market and then the making of some rather subjective judgments. The realities of the local labor market can be ascertained from a variety of sources. The unemployment rate is usually available as a published statistic. The occupations of the unemployed, as noted in Chapter 6, can often be inferred from data on unemployment recipients or from job-applicant data maintained by the local employment service. Some demographic data on the unemployed may be available from the same source. Unemployment rates by age and race are difficult to develop for small areas but may sometimes be inferred from census data. For example, if the question involved the unemployment rate among the black population, and no direct data were available, a course estimate might be made from census-tract data by regressing unemployment rate against blacks as percentage of population.

Alternatively, national ratios may be applied to fill in gaps in local data.[12] The results are not likely to be particularly accurate, but they may be useful if no better source is available.

Labor-force participation rates by age, sex, and race are available from the decennial census. For small areas, it may be necessary to estimate these figures from larger-area statistics. For example, for a town, it may be necessary to fall back on county or SMSA data. Obviously, the census provides a snapshot of the situation and the accuracy of this snapshot diminishes with the passage of time. Updating, usually by applying postcensus national trends to the baseline established with census data, may be necessary. Data on personal and family income are also available from the decennial census. Like all census data, these figures start becoming obsolete the day after the census is taken. However, both the shape of the income-distribution curve and the geographic distribution of wealth and poverty often show remarkable stability over time. Thus, so far as relationships, rather than absolute numbers, are concerned, such data are likely to age slowly. Quantitative data may be supplemented with more impressionistic material—interviews with employers, community organizations, public agencies, such as those which administer public assistance, and the state employment service.

The general practice is to define various categories of people who have particular difficulty in the labor market. Age, education, race or ethnic status, family income, and employment status are common bases for defining such groups. When the "universe of need" has been developed, it must be "prioritized" since, inevitably, the manpower agency or prime sponsor will have funds adequate to deal with only a small fraction of those within the universe of need. The process described above is highly subjective. Indeed determining which groups of people are to be defined as needy is subjective, as is the matter of deciding who among those defined as needy is most needy. How is one to determine whether finding jobs for displaced homemakers is more or less urgent than finding jobs for unemployed teenagers? How is one to determine objectively whether discrimination against those under 20 is a more or a less serious matter than discrimination against those past middle age? It can also not be denied that the political strength of the various potential target groups often influences the definition of need. It would be surprising were it not so.

The *Manpower Program Planning Guide* notes that a program may be tuned for "limited focus-maximum impact" or "maximum focus-limited impact." The former means concentration of effort on the most needy segment(s) of the population while the latter means a distribution of resources roughly proportionate to the distribution of defined needs. The manual, though noting these two options, provides no guidance as to which one to choose. To one comfortable with the marginal approach of microeconomics, both may seem to be suboptimal, for neither suggests the maximizing effect of allocating dollars on the basis of marginal effect. But marginal solutions may violate notions of equity. Assume that the marginal funding approach produces a pattern of expenditure that neither distributes funds proportionately among the various needy groups nor concentrates among the most needy. It may satisfy the economists' conception of efficiency, but may quickly melt in the heat of public discussion.

Having once established priorities for the allocation of funding, there is the matter of evaluating potential employment opportunities. One suggestion is: Set up a point-scoring system in which the number of job opportunities believed to exist and the wage per job (or wage above some stated minimum) are counted as positive factors and the length of training is counted as a negative factor. If there is reason to believe that completion rates for different programs will vary, then a weighting factor might be added for this, too. Though giving the process a quantitative bent, such schemes do not really eliminate subjectivity, for the relative weighting of different factors is still decided on an intuitive basis. But they are useful in that they do make the process more systematic and force the planner to make his thinking more explicit.

When needs and opportunities have been examined and the status of present efforts has been thought through, the process of program design and implementation begins. No discussion of that is included here. Instead, the reader is referred to the *Manpower Program Planning Guide* and to the texts on manpower listed in the Bibliography.

Program evaluation is suggested by the guide as a means of continuously monitoring and adjusting the program. A variety of program evaluation techniques, none of them entirely satisfactory, has been developed. One is to compare earnings subsequent to training programs for those who finished the programs with those who dropped out. The differential is considered to be the effect of the program. This figure can then be compared to program costs to establish a cost/benefit ratio. The very questionable assumption here is that those who complete the program are comparable to those who drop out. This conceptual weakness has not passed unnoticed among those concerned with manpower planning. Another approach is to project the earnings that program participants would have had in the absence of the program and compare them with their earnings some time after the program is completed. As in the above, the differential is taken as the program benefit and laid off against program costs to establish a benefit/cost ratio. A third variation on the theme is to compare program graduates' earnings with those of a matched sample (using age, race, education, and other personal characteristics) who did not participate in the program. Again, the differential is taken as the benefit. The approach has considerable logic to recommend it, but the reader should be mindful of the practical difficulty in constructing the control group. Still another approach is to compare postprogram earnings of graduates of the program with the earnings of those denied admission to the program. This approach would be statistically sound only if those accepted were selected, by a random process, out of a larger applicant pool—a situation not likely to occur often.

Beyond all of the above, there looms a theoretical problem not at all easily resolved. It is the zero-sum-game question noted previously in another connection. If one views the number of jobs as fixed and the search for a job as a race, does training simply alter the order of finishing without changing the number of winners and losers? Or is it possible that manpower programs do produce net gains by improving labor-force quality and making the economy generally more productive? Do the benefits of manpower training problems vary with the state of the economy, perhaps rising in times of low unemployment and falling in times of high unemployment (where the zero-sum-game argument is harder to counter)? This writer advances no answer to these questions. Magnum and Snedeker, in a text on manpower planning, state:

> Manpower policies are disaggregative, "particularistic," and selective; they operate primarily on the supply side of the market and function in the local labor market context. In contrast, fiscal and monetary policies operate on aggregate demand, are broad-gauge and diffused in their impact, and operate in the context of the national economy. While manpower, fiscal, and monetary policies are all directed at full employment, economic growth, and price stability goals, the impacts of local manpower policies cannot be measured by the direct indicators of these goals. This is due in part to the relatively small size of manpower programs. More important is the fact that adequate labor market theory for accounting for displacement effects on non-participants is not yet available.[13]

In a similar vein, the quote Scanlon et al.:

> To be able to speak of effectiveness in meeting a goal requires that the goal and the intervention designed to achieve it be related in some common system of measurement. . . . [G]iven the present state of knowledge, the most appropriate framework for this measurement at present is not the national economy or the target groups in the labor market, but the success of the applicant in the labor market.

When all is said and done regarding the theory of manpower planning, practical matters weigh very heavily. Manpower planners and the administrators and politicians they serve are strongly influenced by the prospects of success and the avoidance of embarrassment. At one time when the writer participated in the planning stage of a manpower planning program, it was suggested that a licensed practical nurse (LPN) program be run. Such programs had been run before, the training slots had always been filled, and the graduates had gotten jobs. Given the locale of the program, it was understood that most trainees would be black women.

The writer was mindful of the fact that among black females, labor-force participation rates were substantially higher than among whites, while male participation rates among blacks were much lower than among whites. He also reflected on the view, widely held at the time, that much of the instability of family structure among blacks was related to employment difficulties of black males. He thus made the obvious suggestion that perhaps a program which would attract primarily black men—featuring welding, auto repair, sheet-metal fabrication, etc.—might be considered instead. The response was simply, but definitively, "But we know we can fill the LPN program." Thus, the subject was settled.

Manpower Terminology

This section contains definitions of the terms used previously and a few observations thereon.

- Unemployment rate—Unemployed ÷ (unemployed + employed) × 100. In this usage, employed means one is gainfully employed for one hour a week or more; unemployed means not working but actively seeking work.
- Labor-force participation rate—persons in labor force ÷ population × 100. The labor force includes both the employed and unemployed as defined above. Participation rates can be computed for any population subgroup for which statistics are available.
- Cyclical unemployment—unemployment attributable to changes in the total amount of employment, resulting from the workings of the business cycle.
- Frictional unemployment—unemployment attributable to the normal mobility of workers.
- Structural unemployment—unemployment attributable to a mismatch between the supply of labor and the demand for labor. Such a mismatch might be related to matters of skill, experience, or physical location.
- Underemployment or subemployment: A number of writers argue that the employment rate presents an incomplete picture of labor market failure. It has been suggested that the underemployment or subemployment figure not only includes the unemployed but also involuntary part-time workers (i.e., those who would work full time if they could) and discouraged workers (see below). In some instances, it has also been suggested that those working at below some specified wage level also be counted in computing the underemployment or subemployment index.[14]
- Discouraged workers—those who have ceased looking for work and are therefore no longer counted as unemployed.
- Economically disadvantaged—as defined by the Department of Labor (DOL) for purposes of CETA eligibility, a member of a family receiving public assistance or eligible for public assistance, or with an income below the poverty

level. A number of other criteria relating to handicaps and institutionalization are also listed by DOL.

The reader will note that for those other than the employed, whose situation is relatively unambiguous, the basis for statistics are rather spongy. Being unemployed (i.e., seeking work) is a self-defined condition. Being a discouraged worker is even more uncertain. "Would you look for work if you thought you could find work?" is indeed a hypothetical question. Labor-force participation rates are subject to some variation. In times of increasing unemployment, the ranks of discouraged workers may grow, moderating the rise in the measured unemployment rate. Conversely, as labor markets tighten, discouraged workers may come back into the market, slowing the fall in the unemployment rate as measured. In addition to varying somewhat with the business cycle, there is long-term variation in labor-force participation rates as well. The most widely noted change in recent years has been the remarkable increase in female labor-force participation, from 37.1 percent in 1960 to 49.3 percent in 1978.[15]

With regard to the types of unemployment, the distinctions between cyclical, frictional, and structural are clear conceptually. In reality, they blur somewhat. The worker laid off because the demand for cars has fallen may be regarded as cyclically unemployed if one regards the fall in demand as a result of the 1980 recession. But if one regards the lowered demand as a permanent condition, then perhaps he is structurally unemployed. If he is cyclically unemployed the day he is laid off, but fails to find other employment in six months, do we then classify him as structurally unemployed?

NOTES

1. Robert Jerrett III and Thomas A. Barocci, *Public Works, Government Spending, and Job Creation*, Praeger, New York, 1979.

2. Ibid. Unemployment declined from approximately 14 percent in 1940 to approximately 2 percent in 1943. Calculations are from *Statistical Abstract of the United States*, Bureau of the Census, Dept. of Commerce, Washington, D.C.

3. Garth L. Mangum, *Employability, Employment and Income*, Olympus Publishing Co., Salt Lake City, 1976.

4. One way this argument can be put is to state that if the match between the abilities of the labor force and the needs of employers can be improved, then labor shortages will begin occurring at lower unemployment rates than would otherwise be the case. Thus, upward pressure on wages and hence on prices generally will not become noticeable until somewhat lower unemployment rates have been reached.

5. This return of power to the states was consistent with the new federalism of the Nixon administration, under which the autonomy of local and state government was to be increased.

6. Those municipalities not large enough to be prime sponsors on their own and not enrolled in consortia may be included in a balance-of-the-state group. Units of government

with populations under 100,000, and not enrolled in consortia, may also be designated as prime sponsors under certain circumstances.

7. PL 95-29.

8. PL 95-524.

9. U.S. Dept. of Labor, press release February 1, 1979.

10. Quoted passages are taken from U.S. Dept. of Labor, "Program Fact Sheet, CETA: A Thumbnail Sketch by Titles," December 1978. Further details can be found in the legislation itself (PL 95-424) and in the *Federal Register*, vol. 45, no. 99, May 20, 1980.

11. U.S. Dept. of Labor, *Manpower Program Planning Guide*, Washington, D.C., 1974. This document is still regarded by the department as the basic how-to-do-it guide for manpower planning committees.

12. For example, if the question were the rate of unemployment among teenagers, one might assume that the ratio of the teenage unemployment rate nationally to the overall unemployment rate nationally was the same as the ratio of those rates locally.

13. Garth Mangum and David Snedeker, *Manpower Planning for Local Labor Markets*, Olympus Publishing Co., Salt Lake City, 1974, p. 185

14. For a discussion of this point see Sar A. Levitan and R. Taggart, "Employment and Earnings Inadequacy: A Measure of Worker Welfare," *Monthly Labor Review*, October 1973, and Julius Shishkin, "Problems in Measuring Employment," *Monthly Labor Review*, August, 1975.

15. *Statistical Abstract of the United States*, 1979, Dept. of Commerce, Bureau of the Census, Washnington, D.C.

12

LABOR MARKET AND FISCAL IMPACTS OF DEVELOPMENT

In many cases, development programs are undertaken without a serious effort made to estimate the effects upon the community. Often, it is simply assumed that the net effects of development upon personal income, the public, and the general climate of business will be good. Once a program is under way, there is often such political and institutional force behind bringing projects to fruition that either it is assumed that the net benefits of any specific project must be positive or the question of net effect is never seriously raised. If it is assumed that economic development, in general, is good, then it is also often assumed that any particular project—unless there are obvious indications to the contrary—is also good.

A large literature on the effects of local economic development has come into being in recent years. In many ways, however, it is not a very satisfying literature. It is primarily a case-history literature. Communities differ widely in the characteristics which affect the impact of any given project, and relevant characteristics of different firms and different projects also differ greatly. Thus, some studies will show significant increases in personal or family income as a result of new development while others will not. Some will show significant municipal fiscal gain from new development and others will not. Some will show significant reductions in unemployment while others will not.

Most studies of development impact have been done for small towns, small cities, or rural areas. The prototypical study is a before-and-after study of the effect of a new manufacturing firm on a small, relatively isolated community. Methodologically, such studies are much cleaner and more defensible than would be true of a comparable study of a large city or of a suburban area made up of a large number of contiguous communities; the utility of such studies outside of the small-town or rural-county context is necessarily reduced.

Despite all of the above limitations, however, a review of development impacts is still useful. If it cannot be shown that net benefits will be positive, it is hard to justify beginning a program. Once the program is initiated, it seems reasonable to look at individual projects in terms of net effects upon the community. Where public money is requested to subsidize development, a minimal condition should show that estimated benefits exceed estimated costs by at least the extent of the subsidy.

Since export-base theory gives primacy to manufacturing, let us consider the factors which might affect the impact of a new manufacuring plant upon a community.

LABOR MARKET EFFECTS

A new plant should exert upward pressure on wages in the community by increasing the demand for labor. In fact, unless one postulates an infinitely elastic supply of labor (the perfect mobility of the classical competitive model), it is hard to argue that there will not be some elevating effect. Even if the plant lowers average wages through a job mix which commands lower wages than the existing job mix, it should still exert some upward pressure on the wages for most job categories.

How large the wage effects of new economic activity are will depend on a number of factors. These include:

- the size of the new plant's labor needs relative to the labor market;
- the availability of labor from outside the municipality;
- the capacity of the municipality and its environs to absorb inmigrants.
- the match between the plant's labor needs and the characteristics of the area labor force.
- unemployment, underemployment, and labor-force participation rates in the area;
- the size of the expected employment multiplier.

All other things being equal, the larger the new facility, with respect to the area labor force, the larger will be the wage effect. Conversely, the greater the availability of labor from outside the area, the smaller will be the effect. The greater the ability of the municipality or its environs to absorb migrants, the smaller will be the wage effect because new households will augment the labor force and relieve the upward pressure on wages. The greater the mismatch between the plant's labor needs and the skills and experience available on the local labor market, the more likely is the plant to hire from outside, and the smaller the general effect on the local labor market is likely to be. If the wages of specialized workers from outside the area are substantially higher than the average of local wages, the plant may raise the area average wage considerably without appreciably raising the wages of the original area residents. The comments by Thompson quoted in Chapter 1 are relevant here as well.

If the local labor market is soft originally (high unemployment, underemployment, or low labor-force participation rates), the wage-elevating effects are likely to be smaller than if the market is tight. The reader familiar with macroeconomics may note the resemblance to the reasoning behind the Phillips curve. Where excess capacity is great, increases in demand result primarily in increased output. As excess capacity falls, increases in demand begin having larger and larger price effects. If one substitutes "employment" for "output" and "wage" for "price," then one has produced a labor market analogy to the traditional Phillips curve. All other things being equal, the larger the multiplier, the larger the wage effect should be.

Summers et al. cite a number of studies indicating that in small communities, new manufacturing activity does raise real median family income.[1] The spread in percentage increases varies very widely. How much, if any, of this effect is to be accounted for on the basis of upward pressure on wages is not known. A new plant might raise median family income by providing jobs paying higher-than-average wages to new residents. This would raise average income levels but not benefit the original residents. In fact, by increasing the pressure on prices within the local economy, it might actually injure them. A new plant might raise median family income by increasing labor-force participation rates, thus increasing the average number of wage earners per family, in the absence of any visible elevating effect upon wages. In brief, it seems fairly clear that new industry does increase average or median income in small places, but the components of this increase are not clear. This writer suspects that studies designed to separate this effect into its components would show large effects from direct wage- and labor-force participation rate factors and smaller effects from the elevation of wage levels for particular types of work. However, at present this must remain only a supposition.

Economic development is often advocated as a cure for local unemployment. The effects of new facilities on unemployment are thus of considerable interest. Both the availability of labor from outside the area and the ability of the area to absorb inmigrants will reduce the effect upon unemployment. The match between the skill needs of the new facility and the skills of the unemployed will also be a factor. Evidently, the better the match, the greater the effect will be. A new plant which increases the demand for nuclear-instrumentation technicians will have virtually no direct effect upon the unemployment rate among coal miners.

A series of studies cited by Summers et al. showed a range of 1.0 to 43.0 for the percentage of new-plant jobs filled by previously unemployed workers.[2] They use the term "unemployed" in its literal meaning rather than in the formal sense of Chapter 11. Thus, some of the unemployed workers hired may have been outside the labor force. Therefore the measured decreases in unemployment would be even smaller. The large spread in the percentages cited should make one cautious about the efficacy of economic development as a cure for unemployment. Even greater caution is probably advisable in advocating economic development as a cure for welfare dependency.[3]

A series of four studies cited by Summers et al., on the poverty status of workers hired by new plants showed a range of 18.6 to 49.1 for the percentage of newly hired workers who previously had been poor, and a range of 13.3 to 27.2 percent for those workers escaping poverty as a result of being hired.[4] All studies were done in areas in which the initial incidence of poverty was high.

In regard to both of these series of studies, Summers et al. note: "As one would expect, the higher-skill higher-wage firms attract few unemployed or poor individuals who typically lack the qualifications necessary to compete for such jobs. Thus, even in areas with significant rates of unemployment and poverty, new plants may not alleviate these twin problems if the skill level of the surplus labor pool and the new labor demand are not closely matched."

For the economic developer, insight into the above effects may present something of a dilemma. His bringing in a prestigious corporate headquarters or research and development operation may bring the approbation of the citizenry who pay his salary but do little for the poor and the unemployed in his and adjacent communites. His bringing in a low-skill assembly operation may do a great deal more for the unemployed and the poor but considerably less for the economic developer's reputation among his future employers. Perhaps this takes us back to Chapter 8 and suggests the value of a public-relations effort which educates the public about the rationale behind the development program. It suggests again that the definition of "desirable" development may be quite different if labor market goals are primary than if tax relief goals are primary.

Multiplier Effect

Beyond the direct effects of a new plant, a multiplier effect should be expected. The argument behind this statement is explained in Appendix A. The multiplier simply expresses the relationship between the number of jobs in the new facility and the total increase in employment in the area resulting from the presence of the new facility. A multiplier of 1.0 would mean that total employment increased by exactly the number of jobs in the new facility, i.e., that on a net basis, no new jobs were created in the secondary or nonbasic sector. A multiplier of 2.0 would indicate that for each job in the new facility, one new job was created in the secondary sector.

Multiplier effects vary considerably. Some of the causes of variations are listed below:

- the size of the area, both physical and economic;
- the degree of linkage between the newly acquired export industry and existing firms;
- the wage pattern generated by the new plant;
- the degree of overcapacity in the secondary sector;
- supply-side limitations in the secondary sector.

Physical size will be important in that, all other things being equal, more of the income generated by a new facility will be spent locally in a large area than in a small area. On the average, the resident of a large place will live further from the nearest border than the average resident of a small place, and this will tend to reduce the leakage of expenditures on many items. Secondly, all other things being equal, a larger jurisdiction is likely to be the place of residence of a higher percentage of a new plant's employees than is a smaller place. This, again, reduces leakages.

Greater economic size implies a larger multiplier because the greater range of goods and services within the area reduces the leakage due to imports. This should apply both to purchases by individuals and by the new firm itself.

The observvation that large places are likely to have larger multipliers than small places not only appears reasonable, but would appear to be sustained by national experience, where, in contrast to subnational areas, exports are well documented. For the United States, exports are about 8 percent of gross domestic product (GDP). For France, they are about 21 percent. For a still smaller country, Belgium, they are about 47 percent of GDP.[5]

The degree of linkage between the new firm and existing industry also affects the multiplier. The more purchases the new firm can make from area firms, the less is the leakage through imports and the greater is the multiplier.

The wage pattern of the new industry also affects the multiplier. The multiplier is calculated on the basis of employment change, but the gain in secondary-sector employment is a function of additional money spent. Therefore, there should be a positive relationship between average wages in the new industry and the increase in secondary-sector employment.

Excess capacity in the local sector may reduce the size of the export multiplier by soaking up increased demand from new export-sector activity without requiring many new workers or new establishments.[6] (An extension of this argument is that successive increments in export-sector growth might produce successively larger multipliers as overcapacity in the local sector was reduced. To the best of the writer's knowledge, this hypothesis has not been tested.) Supply-side limitations in the local sector may limit the size of the multiplier by sending much of the new income off as increased imports.

Finally, if the political jurisdiction in which the multiplier is being calculated is substantially smaller than the real economic area into which the new firm has moved, some of the multiplier effect will occur outside that jurisdiction's boundaries.

Summers et al. summarize a group of studies of new industry in relatively small places.[7] Multipliers for these range from 1.0 to 1.71, with relatively few over 1.50. For the five communities studied by Garrison, the combined multiplier is only 1.08.[8]

For places other than the isolated community for which most impact studies have been done, the literature does not offer too much useful guidance for estimating multipliers. For the very small community which is part of a larger metropolitan area (the town in the suburbs of a major city, for example), a practical course may simply be to assume a multiplier of 1 for jobs within the community and close to 0 for the number of employed residents. Here one assumes that the jurisdiction is so small, relative to the real economic area in which the firm is locating, that almost all payments will leak off as exports. One also assumes that the labor market is so large, relative to the community, that only a trivial percentage of new plant employees will live in the community.

For the case of a large city or an SMSA, the matter is not so easily disposed of. For a city whose economy is stagnant, Garrison's argument regarding secondary-sector overcapacity is probably relevant even though he developed the argument for a very different type of community. Another factor predisposing to an actual multiplier smaller than the calculated multiplier is the rather large share—about one dollar in eight—of personal income in the United States which comes from transfers rather than employment. The calculated multiplier treats all secondary employment as if it were sustained by the earnings associated with export-sector employment.[9] But, in fact, a substantial share of secondary-sector employment is actually sustained by transfers unrelated to export-sector activity.

On the other hand, it is conceivable that some industries which had very strong linkages to existing economic activity or very high wage patterns might produce multiplier effects exceeding the calculated multiplier for the region. On balance, the writer suspects it would be prudent to assume a multiplier for most activities that is somewhat less than that calculated from the place's employment statistics. Unfortunately, the existing literature does not shed much light on this question.

For export-sector activity, it seems reasonable to assume that multipliers will rarely fall below 1.0. Even though export activity may not create new jobs, it is difficult to believe that in many cases it will drive out existing secondary jobs. However, when we turn to secondary-sector development, multipliers of less than 1.0 appear quite probable. A new shopping center, for example, might be expected to have a multiplier of less than 1.0 if most of its sales are taken from existing local stores. Some of the gain in total employment from the new center may be cancelled if competing establishments lay off workers as a result of declining sales. The same might be true for many types of service businesses. The economic developer ought to be very leery of using public funds to subsidize such secondary activity.[10] Unfortunately, the distinction between export and secondary activity, though quite clear to one with a passing acquaintance with export-base theory, may not be too easy to elucidate in public discussion.

FISCAL IMPACT

Studies of the fiscal impact of new development yield a wide range of results. Most seem to suggest some fiscal gains, generally modest, from economic development. As in the case of studies cited earlier, most have been done for small communities where the methodological problems are manageable. Summers et al. summarize a number of these studies and furnish an extensive bibliography of others.[11]

The variation in study results is not surprising when one considers the range of factors which will affect fiscal impact. A far-from-complete list includes:

- taxable value of the development;
- tax structure of the municipality;
- amount and character of residential development caused by new economic development
- amount of excess capacity in municipal infrastructure;
- subsidization, if any, from municipal sources;
- changes in fiscal relations with other levels of government.

Since most communities rely heavily on the property tax, the assessed value of the new facility is a key element in any cost/revenue study. The tax structure of the municipality is also relevant. A community with steep property taxes and no sales tax might find a particular office development to be fiscally superior to a particular shopping center, while a community with a moderate property-tax rate and a sales tax might find the shopping center more advantageous.

Perhaps most important in the majority of cases is the amount of residential development to be expected as a result of new commercial development. If a jurisdiction is very small with regard to the economic area and labor market in which it is located (the suburban town in a large metropolitan area, for example), it may be that no population growth can be attributed to the project. Most workers at the facility will live outside the jurisdiction and, in any case, the community's housing market will be dominated by regionwide or areawide events rather than by events internal to that municipality. In such an instance, most types of commercial development will show a surplus of revenues over costs. This is true simply because most costs of government are related to resident population. It may be that if the development is viewed at a geographic scale sufficiently large to capture the associated population gain, the surplus will vanish. But such a calculation is of little concern to the jurisdiction in question. Much of what might be termed the "suburban land-use game" consists of the effort by communities to capture the revenues of commercial development while shifting the costs of serving the additional population to other communities. The corporate headquarters isolated in a sea of one-acre, single-family zoning is an example of the successful playing of this game. The municipality captures the property-tax revenues but shifts the associated population-serving expenses.

Given that a community must accept some population growth in connection with economic growth, one determinant of the fiscal outcome is the character of the growth accepted. In general, the more affluent the incoming population, the greater the likelihood of a fiscal surplus occurring. This is true simply because a more affluent population will tend to live in more expensive housing, thus paying more in property taxes, and will spend more, yielding more in sales taxes. On the other hand, the costs of providing services are not likely to rise in direct proportion to personal income. For example, an affluent population will not necessarily impose a greater pupil load on the school system than will an equivalent number of less prosperous households.

It may be, however, that on occasion, an incoming population substantially more prosperous than the original population may simultaneously pay its own, or more than its own, share of taxes but still push up the tax rate for the original residents by demanding a higher level of public services. This phenomenon has been noted in connection with rapid suburban growth.

How much, if any, control the community will have over the nature of population growth induced by economic development will vary tremendously. For a rural county with a large supply of buildable land and not much of a planning tradition, there is likely to be little if any control. For a suburban town with limited vacant land and a history of strong land-use controls, the ability to determine the nature of the incoming population may be very great.

The question of excess capacity in municipal infrastructure is important because it bears upon the matter of whether the unit costs of additional services will be higher or lower than the present level of unit costs. In economists' terms, it bears on the question of whether marginal costs will be greater or less than average costs.

For example, if there is excess capacity in the municipal water system so that new development can be served without significant capital investment, marginal costs are likely to be lower than average costs. If the existing rate, including both debt-service and operating costs, is maintained, the increase in revenues will exceed the increase in costs. Conversely, if the system is at capacity so that new demand will necessitate new capital investment, marginal costs will exceed average costs. In this case, without an upward adjustment in rate, a loss will be produced. (It is assumed here that the rate presently just covers total costs.)

The same point might be made with regard to public education. If new students can be accommodated in the existing physical plant, per-pupil costs of operating the system will decline. Total costs presumably consist of some fixed and some variable items. If new pupils increase only the variable component, the average total cost per pupil should go down. If class sizes are below the mandated level, new pupils may be accommodated with little increase in variable costs, another way in which excess capacity causes marginal costs to be lower than average costs. On the other hand, if the system is at capacity and additional pupils force new construction upon the district, it may be that marginal costs will exceed average costs. Comparable comments can be made with regard to other public infrastructure.

The Costing Question

One question which needs to be thought out in doing a fiscal-impact assessment is whether marginal or average costing is appropriate. Assume, for example, that a proposed new commercial development and its associated residential development will use up most of the excess capacity in the water system but are not expected to require significant new investment. If a marginal approach is used, this development will show very low costs. However, the next development will force the community into new capital investments (because the excess capacity will be gone) and show very high costs. A similar comment might be made with regard to the school system. This development might show low marginal costs because the anticipated pupil load can be handled within the existing system, But with excess capacity gone, the next development might show very high marginal costs.

If the decision is to regard the development in question as an isolated event, marginal costing may be appropriate. On the other hand, if the decision is to regard the development as one of a series, an average-costing approach may be more practical. A hard-and-fast rule cannot be offered simply because communities and community situations vary so much. The writer believes that, in most instances, an average-costing approach is more practical.

Degree of Subsidy as a Factor

The degree, if any, of municipal subsidy behind development is a factor which must be considered in assessing fiscal impact. In order to compare the expected net benefit to the community with the proposed subsidy, it is useful to convert all sums into present value. There is no certainty in the present-value technique because of the difficulty in forecasting future revenues, and because different results will be obtained with different discount rates. But it does have the advantage of simplifying matters by putting both costs and revenues into the same terms. As in the use of a common denominator in dealing with fractions, it greatly simplifies thought.

The more difficult problem in dealing with the matter of a municipal subsidy is in determining the probability that the subsidy is the critical factor in causing the development to occur. If one could know the probability, one could multiply the anticipated benefits by some coefficient between 0 and 1 expressing the probability that the development will occur only if the subsidy is offered.

A still more difficult matter is that of determining, given that some subsidy is required, the minimum amount necessary to induce development. There will always be some doubt here. It is in the developer's interest to take the position that the proposition is dubious at best and that only a major subsidy will make the numbers come out right. It is in the municipality's interest to take an opposite position. Obviously, the developer has better insight into his own motivations and financial situation than the municipality can have and, to this extent, has a superior position in the negotiations. Perhaps the path of wisdom for the municipality to take is to acknowledge to itself that it is very unlikely it will be able to offer exactly the necessary minimum. But rather, it is in the municipal interst to cost development out as carefully as possible, with a view to setting a relatively conservative upper limit on the amount it will offer. One consultant who has advised a number of municipalities regarding economic development suggests that the municipality or its consultant simulate on paper the developer's situation and then offer that subsidy it calculates is necessary for the developer to make an adequate rate of return on investment.[12] In this writer's view, the idea has considerable merit but he reserves some skepticism as to how finely it can be done.

Changes in fiscal relationships with other levels of government are matters which should be relatively predictable in advance. Where intergovernmental aid is conditioned by community characteristics (population, per capita value of taxable real property) that will be changed by development, these should be taken into account in the costing process. For example, in New York State, aid to school districts is related inversely to the full value of real property in the district per pupil. Thus, a new facility which increases real taxable value but adds no pupils produces a cut in per-pupil aid. This cut should be subtracted from the school taxes the new facility will pay, before net effect on the school district can be estimated.

Ultimately, the making of the fiscal-impact assessment is an accounting procedure. One adds costs on one side of the ledger and new revenues on the other. When this is done, it is common to recompute the tax rate necessary to sustain the present level of services, in order to convert the absolute dollar figure into a per-household or per-average-taxpayer figure. The procedure differs from some other accounting procedures in the degree of uncertainty which surrounds it and in the number of assumptions upon which it is based. The percentage of new workers that will live in the community, the average assessed value of new houses built to house these workers, the size of the multiplier effect, the percentage of new income generated that will be spent within the community, number of school children the new population will send to the public schools—these are all matters subject to conjecture. No single procedure or municipal-impact worksheet can be provided which will be univerally applicable.

In calculating both costs and revenues, one has a basic choice of either postulating some rate of inflation and adjusting all calculations to it or doing everything in constant dollars. The latter option is much easier and far less likely to lead to confusion. In the past, many communities have walked away from some of the real cost of capital expenditures simply by paying their debts in increasingly depreciated dollars. This is the standard case of unanticipated inflation transferring wealth from creditor to debtor. But given that inflation is now widely anticipated and, presumably, reflected in the structure of long-term interest rates, this process will no longer be as common. This would appear to offer some reassurance to those making the constant-dollar choice. To illustrate the process of making a fiscal-impact study, data for a hypothesized town and project are shown in Table 12.1 and the results of calculations shown in Table 12.2.

Impact of a Hypothetical Project

The reader will note that no time dimension is provided. Various magnitudes shown in the example will follow various time paths to the level shown. The reader will also note that no effects are shown for the construction phase. The writer justifies these two limitations on the grounds that the wise municipal government will take a long view and not be overly concerned with transient events. The approach used is average costing based on present expenditures. In the typology of fiscal-impact techniques suggested by Burchell and Listokin, it would be classified as a modified "per capita multiplier" method. They note that a sample of studies done from 1970 to 1973 indicates that about 70 percent of all fiscal-impact studies use the per capita multiplier. They characterize it as being particularly suitable to communities with populations between 10,000 and 50,000 and with moderate projected population growth.[13]

Before proceeding to calculations, let us note a few salient points.

The relatively large physical size of the town and the distance from the nearest comparable town suggest that much of the labor force for the new facility will live in town. This impression is heightened somewhat by the low population density ($10,000 \div 100 = 100$), which suggests that there is probably a fairly adequate supply of buildable land within the town limits, unless some unusual

TABLE 12.1

Municipal and Project Characteristics

Characteristic	Level
Area	100 square miles
Distance from nearest comparable town	12 miles
Population	10,000
Public school pupils	3,000
Taxable value of real property	$100,000,000
Residential	65,000,000
Commercial and other	35,000,000
Tax rate	$40 per $1,000
Labor force	4,000
Employment in municipality	3,500
Unemployment	6%
Housing stock	3,000 units
Vacancy rate	2%
Composition of employment in town	
Manufacturing	400
Public sector	400
Services	1,000
Trade (retailing and wholesaling)	1,000
Finance, insurance, and real estate	200
Construction and miscellaneous	500
Number of town residents employed in town	2,700
Per capita income	$5,000
Retail sales	$35,000,000
Subject to sales tax	25,000,000
Sales tax collectible by municipality	2%
Total revenues	$12,000,000
Property tax	4,000,000
Assistance from other levels of government	5,000,000
Per capita	200
Per pupil	600
Sales tax	500,000
User charges, fees, and miscellaneous	2,500,000
Total expenditures	$12,000,000
General administration and debt service	500,000
Debt service	500,000
Public safety	1,500,000
Highways and traffic	1,000,000
Utilities	1,000,000
Debt service	600,000
Operating costs	400,000
Parks and recreation	500,000
Social services and miscellaneous	1,000,000
Public schools	6,000,000
Operating expense	5,500,000
Debt service	500,000

Proposed Manufacturing Plant

Nature of operation: Manufacture of high-quality wooden furniture	
Size	300,000 gross square feet
Cost of construction	$25/gross square foot
Average annual wage	$12,500
Gross square feet per employee	500
Estimated annual sales per worker	$35,000
Estimated percent of output subject to sales tax	25

Source: Compiled by the author.

factor, such as steep topography or a very large amount of land in public or institutional ownership, prevails. The nature of the proposed operation (manufacture of fine wood furniture) suggests that a significant number of workers will come from outside the area because of specialized skill requirements, a condition which would not necessarily prevail if the specified operation were, say, assembly of aluminum garden furniture.

The low vacancy rate in the town indicates that there is little slack in the housing inventory to absorb new population and that therefore the inmigration of workers will be accompanied by a corresponding amount of construction.

The size of the retail sales figure, compared with per capita income of the town, suggests that the town is something of a service center for a larger area, since $50 million in personal income is not sufficient to generate $35 million in retail sales. The composition of employment in the town similarly suggests such a role. Note the relatively large employment in trade and services.

The unemployment rate of 6 percent, while not high by present standards (mid-1980), is not extraordinarily low and thus suggests that some workers with commonly found skills can be hired from the local population. The labor-force participation rate of 40 percent ($4,000 \div 10,000$) is lower than the national average and suggests that some local residents may be drawn into the labor force when the new facility begins to hire.[14]

The multiplier effect of the proposed development can only be guessed at. As noted earlier, studies summarized by Summers et al. suggest a range from 1 to about 1.75 for small towns. Given that the town appears to be something of a local center and may have a retailing and service establishment developed beyond the needs of just its own population, let us assume a multiplier somewhat above the average for a small town, say, 1.40.

Consider the probable expansion of the community's population. Assume that interviews with the new plant's management reveal that approximately 300 of the estimated 600 employees will be specialized personnel who will probably have to be recruited from outside the area. This establishes 300 as a minimum number of inmigrating new workers. What about the remaining 540 (300 in the plant and 240 in the secondary sector)?

A drop in the local unemployment rate from 6 to 4 percent would yield 80 workers (4,000 × .02) while still not producing an extraordinarily low unemployment rate. If the labor-force participation rate in the community rose 2 percentage points (somewhat less than half the difference between the present community rate and the national average), another 200 workers would be made available (10,000 × .02). Very conservatively, we might estimate that perhaps 100 additional workers will move in as the spouses and other relatives of the 300 specialized craftsmen mentioned earlier. Thus, an expansion of the employed labor force from local sources by 380 (beyond the 300 craftsmen) can readily be visualized without postulating particularly high labor-force participation rates or excessive tightness in the labor market. If it is further assumed that some labor will be available from the adjacent countryside, the remaining unsatisfied labor needs will shrink further. The assumption of an additional 100 workers, other than the 300 specialized craftsmen, moving into the area to take jobs would appear to be reasonably generous. The reader will note that there is much conjecture here, but given the present state of the art, that is unavoidable. But the alternative—ignoring population growth because it cannot be projected accurately—may give the impression of greater rigorousness but is actually a bigger departure from reality.

Here, it must be noted that much which bears upon the above is particular to each community but is usually quite well known within the community. For smaller places, intuitive impressions may be better guides than the limited published statistics available. For example, it should be known whether the local labor market is generally soft or not. When a local firm seeks to hire nonspecialized workers, is there generally a surplus of applicants or not? Does a substantial percentage of each high school class leave shortly after graduation to seek employment elsewhere? Are there many local women who are not in the labor force but would be happy to take jobs if they were available?

New households in the area should total about 365; of these, 300 represent those of the specialized workers and the remainder, those of the additional unspecialized 100 workers. We assume about 1.5 workers per household for the 100, thus arriving at the figure of 365 rather than 400.

Returning to the tabular data on the community, we note that of the town's labor force of 4,000, 67 percent work in town. Thus, roughly two-thirds of all jobs in town are filled by town residents. Applying the figure of two-thirds to the expected increase in households suggests that an increase of about 250 in the number of households within the town limits is reasonable.[15]

Note, however, that this growth in the number of households will take some years to materialize even though the plant may reach full employment quite shortly. This is because the housing stock of the town will take time to expand. In the short run, the increased demand for housing in the town may drive the vacancy rate down somewhat but many new workers wanting to live in town will have to live outside. With the passage of time, the housing stock of the town will increase and workers will adjust their residence to be closer to work. The rate of construction in town may be limited by the capacity of the local construction industry, by the capacity of the town to provide utilities, or by the rate at which the market absorbs new construction. In any case, one should allow several years for the full population increase to materialize.

Given the figure of 250 new households, we can begin to do some costing. Average household size in the community is 3.4 persons. This is arrived at by dividing total population by the number of occupied housing units. The incoming population is likely to have a somewhat higher household size because it presumably will not include people of retirement age who characteristically have smaller households. Let us assume an average household size of 3.6 for the incoming population. The estimated population gain resulting from the development is thus 900 (250 $\times$ 3.6).

The increase in the school-age population can be approximated. Examination of the community data shows 3,000 school children for 2,960 households. Further, assume that examination of census data shows that of the 2,960 households, 400 have heads 65 or over. If it is assumed that no school children come from such households (probably a reasonably close approximation of the truth), then a figure of 1.17 school children per household with a working-age head appears reasonable. Rounding this to 1.2 and applying it to the expected increase of 250 households would suggest an increase of about 300 in school children.

Cost Estimate

The increase in households, total population, and pupil population now serves as the basis for a number of cost estimates. We begin with public education, the largest item in the municipal budget. Assume there is sufficient overcapacity in the school system's physical plant so that no capital expenditure will be required. This is obviously a matter which would have to be determined individually for any given school district. Nationally, pupil population is declining and will decline for a number of years. In 1963, when the high school seniors of 1980 were born, there were 4,098,000 births in the United States. In 1975, when the kindergarten students of 1980 were born, there were 3,144,000 births. Thus, increasing overcapacity should be the general rule for a number of years to come as the effect of recent low birth rates moves through the age structure of the schools. Given that overcapacity is likely to be increasing for the above reasons and that the full population change will take several years to occur, it may be safe to assume no significant capital expenditures will be required even if the system does not have a full 300-student overcapacity at present.

Turning back to the community data, we see that operating costs for 3,000 pupils are $5,500,500, or $1,833 per pupil. Multiplying this by 300 pupils yields a cost increase of roughly $550,000. Of this, per-pupil aid from the state will defer $180,000, leaving a net cost of $370,000. Note that this calculation is very much of a simplification. There may be some overcapacity in teaching staff, or it may be that though the teaching staff will have to be expanded for the new pupils, the administrative staff will not. Such factors will diminish the actual cost to below that shown above. The economic developer or municipal official making such estimates would do well to contact the school administration regarding such points. (Given recent and projected enrollment declines, the economic developer will find that school superintendents, teachers' unions, and other members of the educational establishment are often strong advocates of housing and economic growth, all for rather evident reasons.)

Let us turn to other costs. A number of studies have suggested that there are relatively few significant economies of scale in the provision of public services and that over a considerable population range, the cost per capita of government shows relatively little change. This suggests average costing unless particular circumstances argue otherwise. Given an expected household size for the new population slightly exceeding that of the present population, doing our calculations on the basis of population increase will produce somewhat higher costs than on the basis of household increase.

For general administration, a 9 percent increase can be anticipated. For public safety, either the same 9 percent increase can be allowed or an attempt can be made to break down the cost of providing police protection into major categories. Assume, for example, that analysis of data such as policemen's logs indicates that 50 percent of operating costs were attributable to protecting residential areas, 30 percent to business and commercial areas, and 20 percent to routine patrolling of rural roads. Then the proportionate increases in population and commercial floor space might be applied to the first two categories while the third category would be assumed to remain constant. For fire protection, if the relative costs of protecting commercial and residential property can be separated, then the relative increases in the number of dwelling units and commercial establishments or in floor space can be used. If not, the percentage increase in the number of housing units can be used.

Somewhat similar comments might be made with regard to expenditures on highways and traffic. If some items which might remain constant can be taken out (perhaps snow plowing and repair of frost damage), then the percentage increase in population can be applied to the rest of the budget. If not, the simple 9 percent population-increase factor can be used.

For water and sewer systems, in contrast to more labor-intensive activities like police protection, it is particularly important to determine whether increased capital investment is necessary. If there is some doubt as to whether the new development will exceed the limits of the existing system and thus force new investment, it is wise to assume the worst case.

For parks and recreation, it is well to make some determination of whether significant excess capacity exists. If it does, then population increase can be applied only to operating costs. If some expansion is necessary, then operating costs can still be treated as a per capita item and a separate entry made for debt service on anticipated new facilities. For social services, capital expenditures are likely to be a very small portion of total costs. Thus, assuming costs will increase as population does would appear to be adequate. Miscellaneous expenses are also treated on a per capital basis, simply for lack of another method.

Revenue Estimates

Revenues can now be estimated. Again, the estimating is done as if the project and its full effects were in existence at the present time.

Property taxes are easily estimated. We note property-tax revenues of $4 million on a taxable value of $100 million. Thus, the effective rax rate is $40 per $1,000 of full value. The floor area of 300,000 square feet and the cost of construction of $25 per square foot suggest a full value of $7.5 million and a tax yield of $300,000. No allowance is made for land value, because this is presumably, not affected by what is built on it. (As a practical matter, tax yield should not be inferred as casually as suggested here. Taxes per $1,000 of market value often vary considerably from one class of property to another. Then, too, in many jurisdictions, a new structure will pay higher taxes than an older structure of the same market value. In short, a detailed consultation with the town's assessor should be had before reaching conclusions about probable property-tax yield.) Sales tax revenues from the project can be estimated as follows: 600 × $35,000 × .02 × .25 = $105,000. This represents number of workers times output per workers times tax rate times percentage of output subject to tax.

Sales-tax yield from expenditures by workers in the facility are not quite so easily estimated but can be approximated very roughly. The first step is to determine approximately what percentage of personal income is likely to be spent on items subject to sales tax. This requires comparing the distribution of a typical family budget by category with a list of the categories of items subject to sales tax. For the former purpose, typical family budgets prepared by the Bureau of Labor Statistics (BLS) can be used. For the community hypothesized here, the BLS moderate level budget for nonmetropolitan areas would appear the most reasonable choice. For the listing of categories of items, the state department of taxation should be consulted. (Most local sales taxes are add-ons to the state sales tax. That is, the local tax is collected simultaneously with the state tax, and the proceeds, less an administrative charge by the state, are remitted to the locality.) In this instance, one would take the estimated payroll of 600 and multiply it by $12,000 to arrive at a total income figure of $7.2 million. If a review of BLS figures suggests that 30 percent of the typical moderate nonmetropolitan budget is spent on items which are subject to tax, then the tax base is: $7.2 million $\times$ .30 = $2.16 million. This figure is multiplied by the tax rate to obtain the tax yield.

An alternative approach might be to take total sales-tax collections for the state as a percentage of personal income for the state, and from this deduce what percentage of personal income is spent on items subject to sales tax. This should be done for a year ending in 9 since the decennial-census income figures lag behind by one year; that is, 1980-census income figures refer to income in 1979. In doing this, one should be aware of two fine points. One is that census income figures tend to be somewhat lower than other estimates of personal income. Thus, the ratio of taxable sales to personal income may be slightly elevated by this technique. Secondly, and more important, some portion of the state's total sales-tax yield does not come from retail sales. For example, there may be no sales tax on houses but the builder may pay sales taxes on various materials used in constructing houses. This point should be clarified with the state department of taxation and an appropriate adjustment made. The manufacturing plant itself will generate some sales taxes through its own purchases locally of goods and services. Discussion with plant management, about the nature of the plant's inputs, may give some indication of how much the plant will buy from vendors within the town. Necessarily, such an estimate will be very rough.

A similar technique can be applied to the payroll associated with the multiplier effect. The problem is to estimate the average income of the additional secondary-sector workers. One technique is to assume that their incomes will be the same, on the average, as those of other workers in the secondary sector. If local data are not available, an average secondary-worker wage can be developed from census data for a base year. Again, the base year will be a year ending in 9 so that the figure will have to be updated to the present. State or national rates of change by industry will have to be applied to advance the figures from the base year.

When the total expenditure subject to sales tax has been estimated, there remains the question of how much of that expenditure will occur within the jurisdiction in question. This is not much of a problem with large jurisdictions but grows progressively more difficult with small ones. No formula can be substituted for the insight of those who know the locality. If retailing opportunities are scattered more or less homogeneously within the larger area of which the municipality is a part, one might assume that the capture of retail sales will divide roughly as the additional labor force divides its place of residence within and outside the jurisdiction in question. If the jurisdiction in question is a retailing center, one might assume that the ratio will be somewhat higher, i.e., that the jurisdiction will capture more retail sales from new nonresidents than it will lose from new residents. Another approach is a crude gravity-model approach. The term "crude" is used here because the gravity model is simply a mathematical abstraction until it is calibrated—a rather laborious procedure which is not likely to be done for these purposes. The gravity-model concept can be used in a casual way without any attempt at calibration, but it must be understood that the results will be very rough approximations.

The gravity model was developed in the 1920s in connection with retailing and originally referred to as Reilly's Law of Retail Gravitation. It has been greatly elaborated on since, particularly in connection with transportation models. Among retailers, gravity models are still sometimes referred to as Reilly models.

Physically, the force of gravity is proportional to $(M1 \times M2) \div D2$. In words, the force of attraction is proportional to the product of the two masses divided by the square of the distance. By analogy, some human activities might be viewed in a similar light. For example, we might consider square feet of retailing floor space as analogous to M1 and number of households as analogous to M2. The model would then suggest that retailing expenditures by the new population in the retail center would be proportional to the product of households times floor space divided by the square of the distance. Unlike the physical model, however, numerous uncertainties creep in. Not all households are identical, nor are all square feet of retail floor space identical. Then, too, in the physical model, distance is an unambiguous matter. In the shopping model, is distance a matter of straight-line distance, road mileage, or driving time? How much should the distance factor be adjusted for an inconvenience or expense, such as a tollgate. We also note that in the physical model, distance is raised to the second power. But is this the right exponent for a retail sales model? If the correct exponent is 2.5 rather than 2.0, the pattern of sales will differ. These and other uncertainties are dealt with when a gravity model is calibrated from actual trip data.

With these caveats, gravity-model philosophy could be used to estimate sales without calibration. The top line of the expression might use floor space and households. If there are large differences in average household income, the household numbers might be weighted for income differences. Thus, 100 households with an average income of $20,000 would be equivalent to 133 households with an average income of $15,000. In an area in which public transportation is minor, distance might be approximated by driving time. For the exponent, a figure of 2 to 2.5 might be used. The analyst then estimates relative forces of attraction between the various population concentrations and shopping concentrations and assumes that sales will divide up proportionately. As noted above, the process will yield very coarse results. The only thing which can be said in its defense it that no better method may be available.[16]

A brief set of cost and revenue calculations, using some of the concepts discussed above, is shown below. The numbers are based on the data hypothesized in Table 12.2.

The reader will note that the general treatment here is conservative. This is particularly so for taxes on new residential structures (see notes for Table 12.2). But to a lesser degree, it is also true of the treatment of new construction

TABLE 12.2

Community Changes

Change		Amount
1. Total additional jobs		840
Export sector		600
Local sector		240
2. Total increase in wages and salaries		9,600,000
3. Increase in proprietors' income		400,000
4. Increase in wages and salaries to town residents		6,400,000
5. Increase in population		900
6. Increase in households		250
7. Increase in housing stock		250
8. Increase in public school enrollments		300
9. Increase in net educational expenditures (see text)		370,000
10. General administration (.09 $\times$ 500,000)		45,000
11. Public safety		
Police protection	(.09 $\times$ 1,000,000)	90,000
Fire protection	(.08 $\times$ 400,000)	32,000
	(.24 $\times$ 100,000)	24,000
12. Highways and traffic (.09 $\times$ 700,000)		63,000
(.24 $\times$ 300,000)		72,000
13. Utilities		
Capital		100,000
operating (.09 $\times$ $400,000)		36,000
14. Parks and recreation		
Capital (.10 $\times$ 700,000)		70,000
Operating (.09 $\times$ 500,000)		50,000
15. Social services and miscellaneous (.09 $\times$ 1,000,000)		90,000
Total		1,042,000
Additional revenues		
Property taxes		
16. New plant		300,000
17. Other commercial		39,000
18. New residential		217,000
Sales taxes		
19. Expenditures by consumers		40,000
20. Products of new facility		105,000
21. Local purchases by new facility		25,000
		170,000
22. User charges and fees		
New business activity (1,000,000 $\times$ 840/3500)		240,000
New population (1,500,000 $\times$ 900/10,000)		135,000
		375,000
Total		1,101,000

Notes: Calculations for the items above are described below or in the text, as noted.

1. See text.

2. The sum of wages from the new plant (see Table 12.1) and an average wage of $10,000 for new workers in the secondary sector (derived from estimates of the average wage of workers now in the secondary sector). No allowance has been made for wage increases for present workers resulting from the tightening of the local labor market.

3. Made by applying the present ratio of proprietors' income to total personal income.

4. Made by assuming that two-thirds of the new workers (see text) would live in town and that the average wages of new workers living in town and outside town would be the same.

5. See text.

6. See text.

7. It was assumed that the relatively low vacancy rate (2 percent) would not be lowered significantly and that, therefore, the increase in housing units and households would be similar.

8. See text.

9. See text.

10. Per capita assignment of costs.

11. Police-protection costs on a per capita basis (assumes that data to make a fine assignment of costs are not available). Fire-protection costing is on the basis that 80 percent of calls are for residential and 20 percent of calls are for commercial structures, with costs prorated on the basis of percentage increase in dwelling units and employment (as a proxy for commercial floor space). In practice, a better estimate for fire protection might be made on the basis of differential experience with various structure types.

12. It is assumed that municipal officials are able to divide expenditures on a 70/30 basis between noncommercial and commercial traffic. Thus, the population-growth percentage is applied to 70 percent of present expenditures and the employment-growth percentage to 30 percent.

13. For capital expenditures, it is assumed that $1,000,000 in additional plant is required and, as a rule of thumb, annual debt service is taken as 10 percent of investment. Obviously, this relationship will vary with the municipality's bond rating and the state of tax-exempt markets at the time the issue must be floated. For operating expenses, the percentage population increase was applied to current operating expenses.

14. Parks and recreation expense is costed under the assumption of new investment of $700,000, with annual debt service at 10 percent, and that operating expenses can be treated on a per capita basis.

15. Because of their relative labor intensity, social-services expenditures are treated strictly on a per capita basis.

16. See text.

17. It was assumed that half of the additional secondary-sector employment would be absorbed by the more intensive use of existing plant and half would be absorbed in new structures bearing the same assessment per employee (or per work station) as in the town's existing inventory of commercial space. The 400 public-sector employees were subtracted to get a private-sector work force of 3,100. Assume that $25,000,000 of the $35,000,000 in nonresidential tax base is commercial (the remainder being utilities, etc.). Then we have a 3.87 percent increase ($(240 \div 2) \div 3,100$) applied to 25 percent of the tax base.

18. The average assessment per dwelling unit ($3,000 \div 65,000,000$) was applied to the additional 250 dwelling units and multiplied by the tax rate. This is an extremely conservative approach since the overwhelming probability is that newly constructed units will be assessed at a higher average figure than units in the existing stock. Thus, an alternative procedure would be to use the average assessment on recently constructed units.

19. Assume that studies for that part of the state indicate that sales taxes are collected on approximately 30 percent of all personal income. Then two-thirds of the additional wage and salary and proprietors' income is assumed to accrue to town residents. When this figure is mutliplied by the 30 percent figure mentioned above and then by the sales-tax rate, we get $10,000,000 \times .667 \times .3 \times .02 = $40,000. Implicit is the assumption that leakages of out-of-town purchases by residents will be balanced by capture of purchases by nonresidents. For a community which appears to have some net inflow of retail sales (see text), this appears to be a reasonably conservative assumption.

20. This figure is simply sales multiplied by the sales-tax rate and divided by the ratio of total sales to taxable sales. Sales within the state are subject to sales tax while sales out of state are not, and the assumption here (see text) is that three-fourths of sales were expected to be to out-of-state customers.

21. Estimated by interviews with new plant management regarding expected geographic patterns for taxable supply purchases.

22. Assume that of all user charges and other miscellaneous revenues such as fines and license fees $1,500,000 is paid by households and individuals and $1,000,000 by businesses. The percentage increase in population is applied to the former number and the percentage increase in employment, to the latter.

Source: Compiled by the author.

for increased secondary activity. Note also that no allowance was made for the capture of additional retail activity stemming from the stimulation of the economy of contiguous areas. In effect, it was assumed that the multiplier effect stopped occurring at the town line. Finally, no allowance was made for sales taxes from local purchases made by new local-sector business activity.

The reader might also note that if we had simply taken the 9 percent anticipated population growth and applied it to the current town budget, an **expenditure** increase of $1,080,000 would have been indicated, a figure which is unquestionably within the margin of error for the calculated expenditure figure. Given that there appear to be relatively few economies and diseconomies of scale in regard to the provision of municipal services, this result is not surprising.

Note also that compared to the private gains ($10 million in wages and proprietors' income), the gains for the public fisc are extremely small. This is the common experience and the case-study literature on local economic development repeatedly shows it to be the case. If one views the purpose of government as ultimately being the enhancement of the well-being of individuals, this situation should not be cause for distress.

Subsidization

The previous figures for this project suggest a surplus of municipal revenues over costs of about $60,000. Assume that some sensitivity analysis is tried and that the average surplus for a range of reasonable assumptions is also $60,000. This might furnish the basis for evaluating a proposed subsidization. Assume, for example, that municipal officials are reasonably convinced that the plant cannot be brought in without public expenditures of $300,000 for an adequate access road. The figure of $300,000 can then be contrasted with the present value of a stream of $60,000 payments. If a time horizon of 20 years and a discount rate of 10 percent are used, the present value is approximately $450,000. Thus, on a revenue/cost basis, the expenditure would be justified. Of course, one could reasonably argue that where no gain to the public fisc will occur, or even where some loss will occur, subsidization is still desirable on the grounds that private gains outweigh public losses.

Sensitivity Analysis

The above costing procedure is predicated on a variety of assumptions. One useful step is to vary some of the basic assumptions and recompute the figures to see how much the cost and revenue figures change. For example, one might vary the multiplier, the number of school children per household, the percentage of work force which will live in town, to get some notion of the possible range of results. To get extreme values to bound the calculations, one might assume that new new employees will live in town and, on the other hand, that all new employees will be inmigrants and that all will live in town. Given the number of assumptions that go into even a simple model such as the above, this effort to find the boundaries within which the answer will lie appears to be only prudent.

Computer Models

There are numerous computer models which can be used to estimate fiscal impact. Burchell and Listokin list a number of these and provide brief descriptions of each.[17] Given the increasing interest in this subject and the continually decreasing cost of data processing, their number will probably increase in the years to come. In general, use of a computer model will be arranged by contract with a consultant, whether profit making or otherwise. This writer has no complaint about the use of such models by municipal officials but would suggest two main cautions. First, the model should be adequately documented. This does not mean that the user needs to know programming details. In fact, there is no reason why he should. However, he must understand the basic process or algorithm of the model. He should understand the assumptions behind it, the variables that are being used, and how they are treated. To use an expression from another field, the model should not be a black box to the user. To allow it to be so is to risk the use of a model which is inappropriate to the municipality's particular circumstances and to abandon any hope of thinking clearly about the quality of results generated by the model. Ideally, the model should have been used elsewhere and retrospective studies should reflect favorably on it. If not, at least the reasoning behind the model should seem sensible and applicable to the municipality in question. If, on a preliminary run, the model produces results which are wildly at variance with common experience, the user should proceed with great caution. As noted before, many empirical studies have shown modest fiscal surpluses from economic development, as does the preceding worksheet. If a model produced a revenue/cost ratio of, say, 5 to 1, considerable suspicion would be called for.

Secondly, and perhaps most important, the user of such a model should inquire carefully about what input data it requires. For example, one model with which the writer has had experience requires a statement of what percentage of the new facility's labor force will live within the community. This is not an unreasonable or uncommon requirement. But knowing about it forewarns the user that no matter how good the model is, it can never be more accurate than the quality of that assumption.

The importance of understanding the data requirements cannot be overemphasized. Until they are understood, it is not possible to come to an intelligent conclusion about whether or not to use the model. Before buying the creature and taking it home, it is wise to find out what it eats.

The above is not to deride the use of models. The use of the model may clarify thinking in part because of the data demands that it does make. Then, too, models have the advantage that once they are operative, they can be run repetitively. Thus, sensitivity analyses can be done more completely than by using a noncomputer model with its need for tedious calculations. Where different development scenarios are contemplated, computer technology permits the exploration of a mass of possibilities that would be prohibitively laborious by hand.

In a cynical vein, one must say that a final advantage of the use of a computer model is the authority it carries with those who are not sophisticated about modeling and do not understand the extent to which assumptions determine conclusions. Computer printout has an authority which hand calculations do not.

A Note on Asymmetry

Though much research has been done on the effects of plant openings, little has been done on plant closings. From the viewpoint of the economic developer, this is unfortunate because, particularly in urban areas, more time and more effort may be spent on retaining existing industry than in bringing in new industry. Though one might casually assume that the effects of losing a plant would be the mirror image of gaining the equivalent plant, the writer strongly doubts that this is the case. One reason for this doubt is that the migration effects of plant openings and closings are not likely to be symmetrical. People are more likely, at least in the short term, to migrate to take employment than because they have lost employment. The sluggishness with which population adjusts to loss of jobs can be confirmed by looking at both lagging urban areas and long-depressed nonmetropolitan areas. Thus, the damage done to the population in place by the loss of a given number of jobs is likely to exceed the benefits realized by the gain of an equivalent number of jobs. This is simply because, from the position of the original population, much of the benefit from the new jobs will be absorbed by migrants, whereas relatively little of the burden of employment loss will be lifted by the outmigration of the newly unemployed. Returning to the data summarized by Summers et al., the highest figure quoted for hiring the formerly unemployed was 43 percent. Using the term "unemployed" in its informal sense, it is quite easy to visualize a situation where a plant closing increases the local unemployed by almost 100 percent of the number of workers laid off.

The above suggests that if the economic developer regards his prime loyalty as being to the present working (and would-be working) population, a job saved may be better than a job brought in. This brings us to the point, made in earlier chapters, that the existing economic structure should not be neglected in the pursuit of the new and glamorous.

NOTES

1. Gene Summers et al., *Industrial Invasion of Non-Metropolitan America*, Praeger, New York, 1976.

2. Ibid.

3. One reason for this assertion is that a large portion of the welfare population is outside the potential labor force by reason of age or disability.

4. Summers, et al., op. cit.

5. *Statistical Abstract of the United States*, 100th edition, section on comparative international statistics. This argument is not meant to suggest a rigid relationship between size and multiplier, but only a loose and general relationship. Factors such as industry mix, relative degree of self-sufficiency in agriculture and natural resources, will also affect the ratio of exports to GDP.

6. See Charles Garrison, "The Impact of New Industry: An Application of the Economic Base Multiplier to Small Rural Areas," *Land Economics*, 1972, p. 329.

7. Ibid.

8. Ibid. In regard to the low multiplier, Garrison notes that the type of export-sector activity involved—manufacturing with a substantial need for relatively unskilled labor—is likely to select communities in which there is a soft labor market. Thus, for reasons noted in the text, the multiplier effect may be smaller than would normally be the case.

9. By "calculated multiplier" is meant that figure developed by dividing total employment by export-sector employment. This is not a particularly difficult approximation to make. The technique is described in a number of urban- and regional-economics textbooks. See, for example, Edgar M. Hoover, *An Introduction to Regional Economics*, Alfred A. Knopf, New York, 1975.

10. Community development (CD) agencies often spend money on the revitalization of neighborhood retailing, an activity which may be justified in planning terms but which may, for the large municipality, be a zero sum game economically.

11. Summers, op. cit.

12. Claude Gruen, in a presentation at a convention of the American Planning Association (APA) in San Francisco, April 1980.

13. Robert W. Burchell and David Listokin, *The Fiscal Impact Handbook*, Center for Urban Policy Research, New Brunswick, N.J., 1978. The assertion regarding place size stems from the finding of various researchers that per capita cost-of-service curves are often relatively flat for places in this size range. This finding means that within the range, average costs and marginal costs will be similar. This is distinct from the case in which the per capita costs fall with increasing size, in which event marginal costs will be lower than average costs. It is also in contrast to the situation in which per capita costs rise with increases in size, in which case marginal costs will exceed average costs.

14. Nationally, labor-force participation is about 45 percent. Though the below-average participation rate may suggest a substantial slack in the local labor market, one should always be cautious about drawing conclusions from a single statistic. For example, it is conceivable that the low rate might be a function of the population's age structure rather than labor market conditions.

15. As an alternative approach to the question of increase in the number of households, one might simply do the following: The total employment increase of 840 might be reduced to 560 under an assumption that there will be about 1.5 workers per household (a reasonable estimate for households with nonelderly heads). If we then assume that 60 percent of these new 560 households will be within the town, a final figure of about 370 new households within the town is reached. This figure was based on a process of calculation which made no allowance for the filling of some new jobs by people presently resident in the town or its environs. If it is adjusted downward by the estimates of jobs which might be filled locally from decreases in the unemployment rate and increases in labor-force participation, a figure quite close to 250 is arrived at.

16. Other methods of estimating trip distribution, such as the intervening-opportunities method, can also be used. For a discussion of various trip-estimating methods, a text on transportation planning should be consulted. See, for example, Robert L. Creighton, *Urban Transportation Planning*, University of Illinois Press, Chicago, 1970.

17. Ibid.

APPENDIX A:
ECONOMICS FOR
THE ECONOMIC DEVELOPER

It is not necessary to be an economist to be a successful economic developer. Political acumen, ability to communicate with others--particularly bankers, businessmen, and politicians--a knowledge of finance, and a certain personal talent for seeing that one's own light is not hidden under bushel baskets are all more important for success in the field than is formal knowledge of economic theory. Nonetheless, some rudimentary economic concepts are useful, both in formulating the broad program outline and in explaining the program to citizens, businessmen, politicians, and others.

Though what follows is taken from the field of urban economics, it is just as relevant to a small town as to a major metropolitan area. It is simple and inelegant but--this writer believes--useful and reasonably accurate. The picture of the local economy provided is the so-called export-base model.[1]

In looking at the economy of a place, whether it be small town, suburb, city, state or region, one might begin by asking a simple question: From where does the money come? If we consider, let us say, a city, we recognize immediately that the residents consume a great deal which they, themselves, do not produce. In short, they import much of what they consume. How are these imports paid for?

In the most general sense, one must export to be able to import. Urban economists often divide the economy of a place into an export and a local sector. Sometimes the terms "basic" and "nonbasic" are used instead of "export" and "local."

What constitutes the export sector? Obviously, manufacturing is an export activity, with the exception of that share of the output which is sold locally. The same can be said for raw-materials extraction and agriculture. But export activity is not confined to physical products. A corporate headquarters which is sustained by corporate earnings outside the area is just as much an export activity as a factory. One might think of it as exporting decisions, studies, and administration rather than a physical product. Tourism, to the extent that it serves people from outside the area in question, is regarded as an export activity. Business services can be thought of as being part of the local or the export sector, depending upon which they serve. A law firm which devotes half its time to serving the needs of the resident population and half its time to serving the needs of firms engaged in export activity could be regarded as being divided evenly between local sector and export sector.

Retailing is generally regarded as a local-sector activity. But if a retailer sells partly to non-residents, that part of his activity may be regarded as export sector. Thus, a neighborhood grocery store might be regarded as being entirely in the local sector while a department store whose market area extends far beyond the community boundary is partly a local and partly an export-sector activity. Comparable statements can be made about personal services. The key question in determining whether an activity is a local or an export one is: Where does the money which pays for the goods or services it provides originate?

In its most simple formulation, the export-base model consists of an export sector and a local sector of the economy. Local-sector activity is sustained by the money brought into the area by the export sector. When the flow of money into the area from exports is equal to the flow of money out of the area for imports, the area's economy is in equilibrium. If the flow of money in exceeds the flow out, the economy will expand. If the reverse is true, it will contract.[2]

A moment's reflection will suggest that this model grossly oversimplifies matters in that many flows of money out of the area will not be for imports and many flows in will not be for exports. The pension that a retiree receives is not payment for an export, but it sustains the local sector of the economy as do the earnings of a worker in an export industry. Similarly, the taxes a local resident pays to a higher level of government are not payments for an import, but they are still a subtraction from the money available to sustain the local economy.

Most types of payments are readily classified under the following scheme, which lists the various flows of money into and out of the local economy:

Outflows	Inflows
1. Payments for finished goods, semi-finished goods, raw materials, and services from vendors outside the area.	Payments received for exports and for services rendered by area firms and individuals to parties outside the area.
2. Taxes paid to jurisdictions other than the one in question. Includes both direct and indirect and personal and business taxes.	Taxes paid to the jurisdiction by outside individuals and firms.
3. Payments to parties outside the area. Includes rent, interest, royalties, transfers.	Payments by outsiders to local firms and residents. Includes rent, interest, royalties, transfers.
4. Expenditures made by area residents and firms outside the area.	Expenditures may by outsiders within the area for goods and services.

The payment a local manufacturer receives for a product sold to a wholesaler outside the area would be an inflow in category 1. Payments he makes to vendors outside the area for raw materials, components, technical services would be an outflow in category 1. A pension check received by an area resident would be an inflow in category 3. An annuity premium by an area resident to an insurance company outside the area would be an outflow in the same category. Money spent in the area by a tourist would be an inflow in category 4. An expenditure made by a local resident while traveling outside the area would be an outflow in the same category. A new facility built in the area by an outside investor would entail a stream of expenditures classified as an inflow under category 4.

Obviously, many different, but equally valid accounting schemes could be set up. In a closed system of communities, every inflow to one community would be an outflow to another. As in a double-entry bookkeeping system, the two totals would necessarily balance.

Returning to the idea of equilibrium, we noted before that when inflows exceed outflows, the level of activity within the system rises. The reverse is true when outflows exceed inflows. If the economic developer sees his function as that of increasing the total level of activity in the system, then this can be achieved in two general ways: increasing inflows or reducing outflows. Bringing in a new export industry will obviously increase inflows. Helping a local firm to begin manufacturing a product for local consumption that was formerly imported will reduce outflows. Helping a retailer build a facility at which purchases once made outside the area can now be made inside the area will also reduce leakages. But helping a retailer build a facility which will simply take away sales from other retailers within the area is playing a zero sum game.

Urban economists speak of an export multiplier.[3] Presumably, each dollar brought into the area by export activity circulates a certain number of times before it gradually leaks out. This concept is readily transformed into an employment multiplier in which each job in the export sector sustains a certain number of jobs in the local sector. Increases in export-sector employment thus cause larger changes in total employment. The ratio of change in total employment to change in export employment is the multiplier. If the local economy is such that there are very large leakages (perhaps most of what is consumed is not produced locally), the multiplier will be small. If there are fewer leakages, the multiplier will be larger. In a general way, large multipliers are associated with larger places because there is less leakage through imports. This point was discussed in Chapter 12. For reasons also noted in Chapter 12, the dynamic multiplier and the static multiplier may not be the same.[4] The estimation of multiplier size is a technical matter and may be pursued in a number of texts.[5]

NOTES

1. This model is described in a number of texts. See, for example, Allan Winger, *Urban Economics: An Introduction*, Charles E. Merrill Publishing, Columbus, Ohio, 1977.

2. The reader familiar with macroeconomics will note the similarity to the simple Keynesian model. In a two-sector model (firms and households), equilibrium is reached when outflows in the form of savings are equal to inflows in the form of investment. In the three-sector model (government is added), taxes appear as an additional outflow while government expenditures appear as an additional inflow. Again, equilibrium is reached when outflows are equal to inflows.

3. Algebraically, the export multiplier is simply total employment divided by export-sector employment. Conceptually, it is very close to the investment multiplier of Keynesian economics. The smaller the percentage of expenditure which leaks out of the area in the form of payments for imports, transfers to outsiders, etc., the larger will be the multiplier. This is similar to the Keynesian notion that the smaller the propensity to save, the larger will be the investment multiplier.

4. As used here, the static multiplier is that which is obtained by dividing total employment by export-sector employment. The dynamic multiplier is the increase in total employment resulting from an increase in export-sector employment. One might think of the former as an average relationship and the latter as a marginal relationship. Among the reasons for suspecting that the latter may be smaller than the former are the possibility of unused capacity in the the local sector (Garrison, as noted earlier) and the fact that a certain amount of local-sector activity is actually sustained by transfer payments rather than export-sector earnings. This latter point causes the static multiplier to be too large because implicit in its calculation is the assumption that all local-sector activity is derived from the export sector.

5. See, for example, E. M. Hoover, *An Introduction to Regional Economics*, Alfred A. Knopf, New York, 1975.

APPENDIX B:
SOME ELEMENTS OF
REAL ESTATE FINANCE

Depreciation

Depreciation is an allowance against earnings based on the concept that man-made objects lose value over time through physical wear and/or technical obsolescence. Thus, failure to consider the loss of value of the capital used in production would cause income to be overstated and taxes on business income to be too high. Depreciation cannot be claimed against land, for obvious reasons, but it can be claimed against land improvements, which have a measurable service life. Depreciation is a subtraction from taxable income, as illustrated in the following example.

An investor purchases a $500,000 industrial property. Of this sum, $100,000 is allowed for land value and $400,000 for the building itself. The investor depreciates the building to a salvage value of $40,000 over a period of 20 years. He elects to take straight-line depreciation. Thus, in each of the 20 years, he claims a deduction against income of $18,000 ($400,000 - $40,000 ÷ 20). Assuming the investor is in the 50 percent tax bracket, the depreciation increases his after-tax income by $9,000 annually. Note that how much depreciation is worth is a function of the tax status of the party claiming depreciation.

Assume that after ten years, the investor sells the property for $400,000. The property has been depreciated to $320,000 ($500,000 - 10 × $18,000) and he will therefore be required to pay a tax on a capital gain of $80,000. Thus, IRS will recover part of the extra income he has received through the taking of depreciation because there would otherwise have been no capital-gains tax in this instance. However, the taking of depreciation is still worthwhile for several reasons. The investor has had the use of the increased income in the ten years between purchase and sale. In addition, capital gains are taxed at a lower rate than other types of income. Then, too, the investor may be able to reduce the size of the tax by timing the sale of his property so that it occurs in a year when his income is low and, therefore, his marginal tax bracket is low.

In some instances, the investor may be able to get his money out of the investment without selling, thus totally avoiding the capital-gains tax (or the increase in the capital-gains tax) to which depreciation may have made him prone. For example, he may refinance the property. A bank or other lender acquires a mortgage on the property and the investor acquires cash. But no sale takes place and hence there is no capital gain to be taxed. This may be done after debt-service payments by the investor have reduced the debt on the property faster than the market value of the property has sunk, or it may be done because an increase in market value (either a real increase or a nominal increase due to inflation) has opened up a larger gap between the value of the property and the value of the underlying debt. Other devices, such as tax-deferred exchanges, may also be available to the investor to postpone payment of taxes.

In addition to the straight-line method discussed above, there are other methods by which depreciation can be taken. Accelerated depreciation permits larger amounts of depreciation to be taken in the first years of ownership.

In general, depreciation is taken by the owner of the property whether or not the owner is also the user. The decision of whether to own or rent may thus be strongly influenced by whether the firm in question is more interested in the tax advantages of ownership or the greater liquidity (less money tied up in equity) of renting.

Leverage

The leverage principle is also referred to as "trading on equity." Two senses in which the term is used follow. When an asset is acquired with borrowed money, changes in the value of the asset produce more than proportionate changes in the value of the owner's equity. Assume an investor buys an industrial property for $500,000, of which $100,000 is his own money and $400,000 is borrowed. At the end of the year, the market for the property has risen and he sells for $600,000 and settles his $400,000 debt. In this case, a 20 percent increase in the value of the asset has been leveraged into a 100 percent return on equity. On the other hand, if the value of the asset declines by 20 percent, the remaining value is equal only to the debt. In this case, a 20 percent decline in value has been leveraged into a 100 percent decline in the value of the owner's equity (from $100,000 to 0). The leverage ratio is then 5 to 1.

Another sense in which the term is used is in relation to the differential between the rate of interest paid for money and the rate of return it earns. Consider the following: An investor purchases a $500,000 industrial building entirely with his own funds. After operating expenses are paid for the year, $750,000 remains. The investor has earned 15 percent on his investment. Assume, instead, the investor purchases the same building with $100,000 of his own money and $400,000 borrowed at 12 percent interest. In the first year, interest on the $400,000 comes to $48,000. Subtracting the $48,000 (an expense he did not formerly have) from the $75,000 leaves $27,000. The investor is now receiving a 27 percent return on his investment.

As in the case before, this process can also run in the other direction. Assume that the return on the building after expenses, but before debt service, is only 10 percent, or $50,000. Debt service will then absorb $48,000, leaving only $2,000 as a return on $100,000 in equity. Thus, the investor will be earning only 2 percent on his investment.

As a general principle, if rate of return on investment exceeds the rate at which funds are borrowed, then the more highly leveraged the investment, the higher will be the return on equity.

Mortgages

Essentially, a mortgage is a loan secured by a lien on real property. The lender, or mortgagee, in addition to receiving a pledge to repay the loan under stated conditions (interest rate, term), also acquires a lien on the property financed. The mortgagee can thus take legal action to acquire possession of the property should the borrower (mortgagor) fail to repay the debt. An instrument which is comparable in principle, but different in legal detail, is the deed of trust. Which of these is used will depend upon the state.

In general, a property cannot be mortgaged for the full amount of its value. Typically, an industrial property might be financed with a 70 percent mortgage and 30 percent owner's or firm's equity. Even though the mortgagee has the right to foreclose on (acquire) the property, loans are made in the expectation that foreclosure will not be necessary. Thus, the biggest consideration in whether or not to make a loan is usually the lender's estimate of the mortgagor's ability to repay.

Where there is more than one mortgage on a property, they are designated as first, second, etc. They differ in the following way: The claims of the second mortgagee, in the event of failure by the mortgagor to repay, are not satisfied until the claims of the first mortgagee have been satisfied. In general, therefore, second mortgages tend to carry somewhat higher interest rates as a compensation for their greater risk.

Second mortgages are granted under a variety of circumstances. In some cases, the seller may grant one in order to make the sale possible. For example, a firm might have 30 percent of the cost of a plant in cash and be able to borrow another 50 percent from a commercial bank. The seller, to prevent the sale from collapsing, might provide the remaining 20 percent. The second mortgage by the seller is sometimes referred to as a purchase-money mortgage and the act of granting one, sometimes referred to as taking back a mortgage.

The term or payment period on conventional mortgages varies considerably. Kinnard and Messner cite 15 to 30 years as being common on new industrial buildings and 10 to 15 years as being common on older buildings.[1] Payout periods in general are shorter on second mortgages than on first mortgages, though there is much variation here. Because of the greater risk associated with second mortgages, it is only natural that second-mortgage lenders be less willing to accept very long payout periods.

The manner of repayment varies considerably from one mortgage instrument to another. In some cases the payments will be adjusted to produce level debt service to the end of the mortgage. A payment of constant size is made through the life of the mortgage. As the principal is repaid, the amount of interest in each succeeding payment is smaller and the amount of principal repayment (amortization) larger. (Home mortgages have normally been done this way, though in the last year or two, some new arrangements have been appearing.)

Another common arrangement is the balloon payment. Payment proceeds until a specified date, at which time all of the unpaid principal becomes due. At this point, the mortgagor either repays from funds put aside against this date or refinances with the same or other institutions. For example, the borrower and lender might agree on level debt-service payments such as would reduce the value of the loan to 0 after 15 years. However, they would also agree that at the end of the tenth year, the remaining debt (about half the original debt) will fall due. Such an arrangement gives the borrower the advantage of the lower debt service that would be associated with a longer-term instrument, while giving the lender assurance that his capital will not be tied up for an unduly long time period.

Present Value

Often, it is useful to convert a stream of future payments into their value as of the present. This might be done, for example, to compare the merits of two possible investments. Or it might be done to compare the cost of an investment with the expected value of its return to determine whether or not the investment is worth taking.

The calculation is made by applying a discount factor to future payments received. For example, if a discount factor of 10 percent is used, a stream of $1,000 payments beginning at the present would have a present-value calculation of $1,000 + $1,000 ÷ 1.10 + $1,000 ÷ (1.10)^2 + $1,000 ÷ (1.10)^3 .... One might think of the discount factor as stemming from a propensity to value the future less heavily than the present, or as a factor inserted for the uncertainty of future events, or as an expression of the idea of interest. In the latter case, one regards $1,000 today as being worth more than $1,000 a year from now because $1,000 invested today will have grown to more than $1,000 at the end of the year. Many books on finance contain present-value tables so that it is not actually necessary to go through the computations shown above to find the present value of a stream of payments.

Sources of Mortgage Funds

The construction of industrial and commercial facilities is financed somewhat differently than the acquisition of existing properties. For this reason, they are discussed separately below. What follows is an extremely brief summary. There is an enormous variety in financing and new financial arrangements are continually appearing.

New construction is generally financed in a two-stage process. Financing is provided by a short-term lender for the construction period. After construction is completed, long-term financing is arranged with another lender and the short-term debt is settled. Commercial banks are the single largest source. In general, lending on construction is regarded as somewhat riskier than lending to purchase an existing structure. Commonly, the amount lent for construction will not exceed 75 percent of market value or 80 to 90 percent of the value of the permanent financing. Construction-loan interest rates are usually fractionally higher than the rates on permanent financing. Generally, the lender will require that a take-out commitment first be obtained. This is a commitment by another institution to advance permanent financing (and hence take the construction lender out of the situation) when construction is completed. In addition, the construction lender may require a performance bond from the builder and will advance construction money in stages, upon successful completion of previous stages. Typically, construction loans are indexed against the prime rate, with rates ranging from a fraction of a point to several points above the prime.

Mortgage companies or mortgage bankers are another source of construction financing. These organizations, which essentially are financial intermediaries between the end user and sources of long-term funds, may also serve to arrange permanent financing.

In recent years, real estate investment trusts (REITs) have become a source of construction funds. These are corporations which pool the funds of a large number of investors to make a variety of real estate loans and investments. They are required to invest most of their funds in real estate and to pay back at least 90 percent of their earnings as dividends to their shareholders. In return for this they receive certain favorable tax treatment. Unlike commercial banks and mortgage companies, REITs often also offer permanent financing.

There are a number of sources of permanent financing. A major source is life insurance companies. In some cases, they may negotiate directly with potential borrowers. In other cases, they may purchase mortgages from mortgage bankers.

Real estate investment trusts, as mentioned above, are a major source of long-term financing. In some cases, they may simply lend money. In other cases, they may also participate by taking some share of profits or rents.

Commercial banks may occasionally serve as a source of long-term credit, though as noted before, they are relatively more important as a source of construction financing.

Pension funds are becoming increasingly important as a source of permanent financing. Like life insurance companies, they have large amounts of cash that must be invested in reasonably secure instruments over long periods of time.

Mortgages on commercial real estate offer them permanence, a reasonable degree of security, and relatively low transaction costs. Thrift institutions such as savings and loans and mutual savings banks are occasionally sources of permanent financing. Very often, because of the size of such financings, they will participate in concert with other lenders. A variety of miscellaneous lenders can also be named. Companies with substantial assets may provide permanent financing through the mechanism of a purchase-money mortgage. That is, a company seeking to sell property may provide second-mortgage financing in order to facilitate the sale. Wealthy individuals may be a source of permanent financing. In many instances they also may participate by means of stock options, and percentage-of-income arrangements. Other institutions such as foundations and university endowment funds may also be sources of permanent financing.

NOTE

1. W. N. Kinnard, and S. D. Messner, *Industrial Real Estate*, 2d ed., Society of Industrial Realtors and National Association of Realtors, Washington, D.C., 1975.

APPENDIX C:
MEMBERSHIP OF THE LEAGUE OF
ECONOMIC DEVELOPMENT
ORGANIZATIONS

American Gas Association, 1515 Wilson Blvd., Arlington, Va. 22209.

American Industrial Development Council, 1207 Grand Ave., Kansas City, Mo. 64106.

Edison Electric Institute, 1111 19th St., N.W., Washington, D.C. 20036.

Great Lakes Area Development Council, 3 West Old State Capitol Plaza, Springfield, Ill. 62701.

Industrial Development Research Council, Peachtree Air Terminal, Atlanta, Ga., 30341.

National Association of Corporate Real Estate Executives, 7799 SW 62 Ave., South Miami, Fla. 33143.

National Association of Development Organizations, 38 Ivy St. S.E., Washington, D.C. 20003.

National Association of Industrial and Office Parks, 1700 N. Moore St., Arlington, Va. 22209.

National Association of State Development Agencies, One Skyline Place, 5205 Leesburg Pike, Falls Church, Va. 22041.

National Council for Urban Economic Development, 1730 K St., N.W., Suite 1009, Washington, D.C. 20006.

Northwestern Industrial Developers Association, Charles Professional Center, Suite 511, Waldorf, Md. 20601.

Pacific Northwest Industrial Development Council, Puget Power Building, Bellevue, Wash. 98009.

Society of Industrial Realtors, 925 15th St., N.W., Washington, D.C. 20005.

Southern Industrial Development Council, Georgia Institute of Technology, Atlanta, Ga. 30332.

Urban Land Institute, 1200 18th St., N.W., Washington, D.C. 20036.

BIBLIOGRAPHY

Below are listed a limited number of books the author believes will be of some practical value to the economic developer. No attempt has been made to include articles. The cited works by Summers, and Reigeluth and Wolman, in particular, contained extended lists of relevant journal articles. The brevity of the public-relations and advertising section is a reflection of the fact that relatively little has been written on this important aspect of local economic development programs.

PUBLIC RELATIONS AND ADVERTISING

Levine, T., "Attracting Industry: The Use and Abuse of Advertising and Promotion," in *Guide to Industrial Development*, Prentice-Hall, Englewood Cliffs, 1972.

Wagner, K. C., *Economic Development Manual*, University of Mississippi Press, Research and Development Center, Jackson, 1978.

DEVELOPMENT PLANNING

Chapin, F. S., and E. J. Kaiser, *Urban Land Use Planning*, University of Illinois Press, Urbana, 1979.

Chiara, J. D., and L. Koppelman, *Planning Design Criteria*, Van Nostrand and Reinhold, New York, 1969.

Creighton, R. L., *Urban Transportation Planning*, University of Illinois Press, Urbana, 1970.

Howard, D., ed., *Guide to Industrial Development*, Prentice-Hall, Englewood Cliffs, 1972.

Ide, E. A., *Estimating and Floor Area Implicit in Employment Projections*, Bureau of Public Roads, U.S. Dept. of Transportation, Washington, D.C., 1970.

Lochmoeller, D. C., et al., *Industrial Development Handbook*, Urban Land Institute, Washington, D.C., 1975.

Moriarty, B. M., *Industrial Location and Community Development*, University of North Carolina Press, Chapel Hill, 1980.

Reigeluth, G. A., and H. Wolman, *The Determinants and Implications of Communities Changing Competitive Advantages: A Review of Literature*, Urban Land Institute, Washington, D.C., 1979.

Travel and Facilities Section, Arizona Dept. of Transportation, in cooperation with Federal Highway Administration, *Trip Generation Intensity Factors*, U.S. Dept. of Transportation, Washington, D.C., 1976.

Tweeten, L., and G. L. Brinkman, *Micropolitan Development*, Iowa State University Press, Ames, 1976.

COMMERCIAL REAL ESTATE FINANCING

Case, F. E., and J. M. Clapp, *Real Estate Financing*, John Wiley and Sons, New York, 1978.

Kinnard, W. N., and S. D. Messner, *Industrial Real Estate*, 2d ed., Society of Industrial Realtors and National Association of Realtors, Washington, D.C., 1975.

Smollen, L. E., and J. Hayes, et al., *Sources of Capital for Community Economic Development*, Center for Community Economic Development, Cambridge, Mass., 1976.

DEVELOPMENT IMPACTS

Burchell, R. W., and D. Listokin, *The Fiscal Impact Handbook*, Center for Urban Policy Research, State University of New Jersey, Rutgers, New Brunswick, 1978.

Christensen, K., *Social Impacts of Land Development*, Urban Institute, Washington, D.C., 1976.

Muller, T., *Economic Impacts of Land Development*, Urban Institute, Washington, D.C., 1976.

Reigeluth, G. A., *Fiscal Consequence of Changes in a Community's Economic Base: A Review of the Literature*, Urban Land Institute, Washington, D.C., 1979.

Sternlieb, G., *Housing Development and Municipal Costs*, Center for Urban Policy Research, State University of New Jersey, Rutgers, New Brunswick, 1973.

Summers, G. F., et al., *Industrial Invasion of Non-Metropolitan America: A Quarter Century of Experience*, Praeger, New York, 1976.

Summers, G. F., and A. Selvik, *Non-Metropolitan Industrial Growth and Community Change*, Lexington Books, D.C. Heath, Lexington, Mass., 1979.

MANPOWER PLANNING

Gordon, D. M., *Theories of Poverty and Unemployment*, Lexington Books, D.C. Heath, Lexington, Mass., 1972.

Mangum, L., *Employability, Employment and Income*, Olympus Publishing, Salt Lake City, 1976.

Mangum, G. L., and D. Snedeker, *Manpower Planning for Local Labor Markets*, Olympus Publishing, Salt Lake City, 1974.

Manpower Program Planning Guide, Manpower Administration, U.S. Dept. of Labor, Washington, D.C., 1973.

URBAN AND REGIONAL ECONOMICS

Hoover, E. M. *An Introduction to Regional Economics*, Alfred A. Knopf, New York, 1975.

Sternlieb, G., and J. W. Hughes, *Post-Industrial America: Metropolitan Decline and Inter-regional Job Shifts*, Center for Urban Policy Research, State University of New Jersey, Rutgers, New Brunswick, 1975.

Thompson, W. R., *A Preface to Urban Economics*, Johns Hopkins Press, Baltimore, 1965.

Tiebout, C. M., *The Community Economic Base Study*, Committee for Economic Development, New York, 1962.

Winger, A. R., *Urban Economics: An Introduction*, Charles E. Merrill Publishing, Columbus, Ohio, 1977.

INDEX

abatement: tax, 20-21, 91-92
advertising, 17-18, 83-87
agricultural technology: effect on
    economic location, 34-35

Burchell, Robert W., 142, 154
building permit data, 61
business services, location of, 57

CETA (Comprehensive Employment
    and Training Administration),
    119-24
Chapin, Stuart, 69
computer models for estimating
    fiscal impact, 154-55
conflict over economic develop-
    ment, 14-16
construction: costs, 54; trends in, 61
corporate headquarters: location, 56
corporate tax abatement, 92
cost of living, 36, 52
crime: impact on economic location,
    51

data base information package,
    87-89
demographic characteristics informa-
    tion, 55
development coalition, 13-14
development planning, 21-22
development cost write downs, 94
Department of Housing and Urban
    Development (see Housing and
    Urban Development)
differential taxation, 36

discouraged workers, 129

economic development: environ-
    mental impact, 7; federal
    assistance to, 96-115;
    planning, 21-22; potential
    for, 44-61; side effects, 6-8
Economic Development Administra-
    tion (EDA), 20, 94, 100-8
economic development agencies:
    functions of, 17-21; legal and
    public powers, 22; opposition,
    14-16; personnel, 25, 27-28;
    political environment, 10-16;
    support building, 13-14; types
    and structures, 23-27
Economic Development District,
    103, 105 (see also Economic
    Development Administration)
economic growth: motivation for
    economic development pro-
    gram, 6; recent geographic
    shifts, 29-31 (see also fiscal
    impact)
economic models: export base, 135-
    38
Economic Stimulus Appropriations
    Act, 120
economically disadvantaged, 129
education as a factor in economic
    location, 50-51
employment, 59-60 (see also unem-
    ployment)
energy: cost, 38, 53; impact on
    location trends, 42

172

ABOUT THE AUTHOR

JOHN M. LEVY has been an associate professor in the Division of Environmental and Urban Systems, Virginia Polytechnic Institute and State University, Blacksburg, Virginia since 1979. Prior to that he was employed for a decade in the planning profession. During part of that period he organized and then operated an economic development agency and a development financing agency for a suburban county in the New York region. He holds a master's degree in economics from Hunter College of the City University of New York and a doctorate in urban public policy studies from New York University.